AF600046

JUDICIAL PROCEDURE IN DISMISSAL OF CLERICAL EXEMPT RELIGIOUS.

A DISSERTATION

SUBMITTED TO THE FACULTY OF SACRED SCIENCES
OF THE
CATHOLIC UNIVERSITY OF AMERICA

IN PARTIAL FULFILLMENT OF THE REQUIREMENTS
FOR THE DEGREE

DOCTOR OF CANON LAW

By the

REV. WENCESLAS CYRILL MICHALICKA O. S. B, J. C. L.,
OF ST. PROCOPIUS ABBEY LISLE, ILLINOIS.

1923.

Permissu Superiorum:

VALENTINE KOHLBECK, O. S. B.,
Abbas-Coad. Abbatiae S. Procopii.

Nihil Obstat:

† THOMAS J. SHAHAN,
Censor Deputatus.

Imprimatur:

† MICHAEL J. CURLEY,
Archiepiscopus Baltimorensis.

Baltimorae, Die XV Maii, 1923.

TABLE OF CONTENTS

INTRODUCTION.

Dismissal was ever a right of religious Orders and congregations. This right is based upon profession itself which is a contract. In consequence of this fact, when one becomes a religious through profession, certain rights and duties arise from this promise between him and the religion entered. He is bound to fulfill his obligations. However, if he neglects to do so through grave imputable violations, this agreement may be severed by excluding him from the religious society.

Religion.—The term here designates any Order or Congregation,—is a society, approved by legitimate ecclesiastical authority, composed of members who are bound by vows and strive for evangelical perfection. If any of the members does something that is to the detriment or harm of the society, there ensues a disturbance that impedes the welfare of that body. Common good of that society demands that the disturbance must be remedied and, if necessary, the cause must be removed.

The obligations assumed by a professed member whether made expressly or implicitly, at least, include that he will conform himself to the Rule and Statutes of the religion. If such a member does not abide by the promise that he had made and thereby causes grave harm to the common good, the religion may use its right and power to dismiss him, if he remains obstinate in his perverse determination. Every society has a natural right to dismiss those members that are harmful to it. The Church exercises this power by severing obstinate members from her communion.

We find this sanctioned by the Popes and Fathers of the Church. Pope Leo, in his seventy-fourth Epistle to Anatolius, states that those, to whom correction is of no avail, are not to be spared from expulsion, "Ut his, quibus prodesse correptio non potuerit, non parcat abscisio. Oportet enim nos evangelici meminisse mandati, quod ab ipsa veritate praecipitur, ut, si oculus, aut pes, aut dextera scandalizaverit manus, a compage corporis auferatur" (1.) St. Jerome, when commenting upon the Epistle of St. Paul to the Galatians c. V, asserts that an infected or deseased member be separated from the rest, lest, the whole be in-

1. C. 34, Caus. 24, q. 3.

fected "Resecandae sunt carnes putridae et scabiosa a caulis ovis repellenda, ne tota domus, massa, corpus et pecora ardeat, corrumpatur, putrescat, intereat " (2.)

Founders of monasticism and religious Orders made provisions in their Rules or Constitutions for expelling or dismissing members. St. Basil writes in his Rule, that the obstinate and incorrigible one, after having been admonished repeatedly, is to be separated from the community of brethren "Ut membrum corruptum et penitus inutile medicorum exemplo, a communi corpore resecare debemus" (3.) Further, he states other transgressions for which penalty of expulsion was given e. g. one, grieving and being angry on account of having been punished, was expelled (4); he who was addicted to an incorrigible vice, after frequent reprimands, was to be expelled (5.)

St. Benedict, in his Rule, commands that the obstinate and incorrigible one be expelled from the community after having been admonished, corrected and punished with excommunication. "Let the Abbot use the sword of separation, as the Apostle saith: "Put away the evil one from among you" (I. Cor. 5); and again: "If the faithless depart, let him depart (I. Cor. 7), lest one diseased sheep infect the whole flock" (6). In like manner, this is found in other authors of Rules and Constitutions, where the right of expelling harmful members is included in the prescriptions e. g. Rule of St. Augustine (7), Constitutions of St. Dominic (8) and others.

In eccesiastical legislation, we find many instances where Pontiffs decreed that religious, if they had been guilty of certain grave transgressions, were to be expelled. For example Innocent III, decreed that those monks, who were found to possess anything unlawfully, after having been admonished in vain, should be expelled; nor were they re-admitted, unless they repented according to the prescribed monastic discipline (9.). Pope Honorius ordained that obstinate and rebellious monks, if they

2. C. 16, Caus. 24, q. 3.
3. Regula Fusius Tractata, 28.
4. Regula Brevius Tractata, 44.
5. Regula Brevius Tractata, 57.
6. Holy Rule, c. 28.
7. Cap. 6.
8. Dist. I, c. 19; Leurenius, Forum Ecclesiasticum, III, 31, q. 853.
9. C. 6, X, III, 35.

continued in their contumacy, were to be punished by expulsion (10). Again Innocent III, ordered that the Canons Regular of a certain monastery should be excommunicated for disobedience to their prior and that, if they remained incorrigible, they were to be expelled from the community (11.) On another occasion it was decreed that certain refractory monks should be expelled and the community reformed, if not from within, then by members of another Order (12).

During the course of time new and definite legislation became necessary in the matter of dismissing religious. The Supreme Pontiffs recognizing this need issued various decrees to this effect. We shall note here briefly some of the decrees which were directly concerned with the matter of expulsion and that defined the mode of procedure for Orders and Congregations up to the New Code.

In the time of Pius IV, the Sacred Congregation of the Council published a number of decrees by his authority which were sent to Procurators General of Orders. These prescribed that ill-willed and incorrigible religious were to be punished, even by incarceration, however, not by expulsion from the Order (13). Those decrees were based upon the opinions of Glossators of the Old Law as Benedict XIV asserts. They interpreted the laws of the Decretals concerning expulsion of religious to mean that members were not to be excluded from the monastery or Order, but, that they were only to be separated from the society of the other Regulars (14). The decisions of these decrees became almost impossible to be observed by the various Orders, wherefore, the Procurators General, during the reign of Urban VIII, presented petitions to change the existing regulations. Wherefore, the Sacred Congregation of Council issued a decree that the incorrigible were to be expelled from Orders after a definite sentence.

In this decree of Urban VIII entitled "Sacra Congregatio" (15) real incorrigibility was required by general law; it an-

10. C. 8, X, III, 35.
11. C. 10, X, I, 33.
12. C. 7, X, III, 50.
13. De Synod. Dioc., Lib. 13, c. 11, n. 15.
14. De Synod, Dioc., Lib. 13, c. 11, n. 15.
15. Decree of S. Congr. Council, Sept. 21, 1624.

nulled all Statutes and Constitutions of whatever Order, even if approved by the Holy See, in this matter. Moreover, it prescribed an incarceration of one year for the incorrigible, if at the end of that time a religious continued to be obstinate, he was expelled after a formal trial. Furthermore, it ordained that the procedure was to be conducted according to the respective style and constitution of each Order, the causes for expulsion were to be proven in accordance with the prescriptions of Sacred Canons. The sentence of expulsion was pronounced by the General with the assent of six Fathers selected from the Order (16).

Upon a repeated demand of the Procurators General to moderate the aforesaid decree of Urban VIII in order to make it less difficult to expell the incorrigible, a new decree was issued under Innocent XII, entitled "Instantibus" (17), which altered some of the prescriptions of the former. The modifications in substance were: a) the year of incarceration was shortened to six months, b) the faculty of expulsion was extended to the Provincials with the assent of six other religious who were approved by the General constituted the tribunal for pronouncing the sentence, c) which required the approval of the General in order to have effect.

The regulations, designated especially by these two decrees of Urban VIII and Innocent XII, although particular prescriptions were issued to individual Religions, were observed by the Orders in general.

The Sacred Congregation of Bishops and Regulars ordained in the decree "Auctis admodum" (18), that the two preceeding decrees "Sacra Congregatio" and "Instantibus" with other general decrees concerning the method of expelling religious remained not only in force, but were extended to Institutes of simple vows. It defined anew the term, incorrigibility, to mean persistence in ill-will after admonitions and corrections had been given by a superior three different times for violations of law. The expulsion of a member followed only after a regular trial. A summary trial was not permitted, unless, a dispensation was granted by this Sacred Congregation.

---

16. Decree "Sacra Congregatio" n. 7.

17. Die 24 July, 1694. (It was a peculiar Congregation on account of a select number of Cardinals designated specially for this case).

18. Nov. 4, 1892.

The final decree, before the codification of the New Law, was issued by the Sacred Congregation of Religious (19) which altered the mode of procedure in expelling and dismissing religious in Orders and Institutes. It gave the reason for doing so. stating that the prescriptions and solemnities of general law, especially, those contained in the decree of Urban VIII, could no longer be observed conveniently in our days, wherefore, it was deemed opportune and more applicable to our times to ordain new laws in this matter (20).

The more notable regulations, which superseded those of the former decrees, were in substance the following: a) the competent tribunal consisted of a Superior General or Abbot General and at least four Counsellors; b) a Promoter of justice was appointed to each tribunal; c) the procedure was a summary one, although, special privileges of any Order or Institute remained in force. It defined what necessarily had to precede a trial and upon what grounds it could be commenced, likewise, stating how it was to be conducted. Provisions were made for instant dismissal in certain very grave cases, when the ordinary formalities were dispensed by general law itself. Then it enumerated particular cases when dismissal was effected by a declaratory sentence of a competent authority. Finally, it prescribed rules for expelling nuns.

The New Code contains definite laws in the matter of dismissing religious. It divides them into three classes viz., the first is concerned with all religious who professed temporal vows; the second includes all religious who are bound by simple vows of clerical non exempt or lay Institutes and the third comprises all religious who have perpetual or solemn vows that are in clerical exempt Orders or Congregations. Religious in the first two classes are dismissed without judicial procedure, those, however, of the third class cannot be dismissed without the prescribed judicial procedure.

The object of this work is to describe the judicial procedure, as it now is observed in the New Law, when religious of simple perpetual or solemn vows in exempt clerical Religions are to be dismissed.

19. "Quum singulae" May 16, 1911.
20. Prologue of the decree "Quum singulae".

DISMISSAL

By dismissal is understood an act of sending away one who has entered a religious community after profession had been pronounced. Etymologically considered, the compound word is derived from two words, "dis" meaning separation or division and "mitto" signifying to send, combined it imports an act of sending one away. In a canonical sense, it denotes that a member professed in a religious institute is sent away from that body with the effect that he is no longer considered a member having either rights or privileges of that body.

In the Old Law, there were distinctions made as to the manner in which members were dismissed. The terms "dismissal" and "expulsion" were used promiscuously; however, these meant two different acts. By dismissal was meant, an act whereby a competent superior, outside of a trial, separated a professed member from a religious Order or Congregation upon ascertaining the fact that there existed certain grave and just causes, although, not necessarily imputable to the member (1). On the other hand, expulsion meant, that a professed member was sent away from a Order or Congregation by a competent superior, after having been tried in an ecclesiastical court, for grave, public and persistent offenses (2).

An important factor, that demanded consideration in the matter of expelling members of religious Orders and Congregations in the Old Law, was the kind of profession such a religious had pronounced. There were different procedures on account of the greater or lesser bond that had to be severed, when a member was dissmissed.

In a short conspectus, we shall see the methods according to which different classes of religious were dismissed. a) Men who had pronounced solemn vows whether in major orders or not were expelled only after a judicial trial that was prescribed by the decrees of Urban VIII, and Innocent XII (3). b) Religious, in Institutes of simple vows, who had pronounced perpetual or temporal vows and in major orders, were dismissed through a

1. Wernz, III, n. 676.
2. Wernz, III, ibid.
3. "Sacra Congregatio" Sept. 21, 1624 and "Instantibus" July 24, 1694.

regular procedure (4). The religious had a right to appeal from the sentence of expulsion within a stated time (5). This appeal had the force of suspending the sentence in the meantime. However, if the religious did not make use of this means, the sentence passed into a "res iudicata" (6), whereby the expulsion took effect.

One expelled remained suspended perpetually "ipso facto", if he were in major orders, and this penalty was reserved to the Holy See (7). The vows were not dispensed by the act of expulsion, but, the religious was under obligation to observe them in as far as it was with his subsequent condition. The vows of obedience and poverty were relaxed; however, the vow of chastity remained in full vigor, unless such an Institute enjoyed a special privilege granted by the Holy See that those dismissed were freed from their vows. c) Religious, not promoted to major orders but simply professed in Orders and Congregations, were dismissed before their solemn vows by the Superior General and his Counsel. The cause for dismissal was grave, just and reasonable. Upon the examination of its existence and verification, the dismissal could be pronounced. These simple vows, which preceded solemn vows, had the effect of perpetuity as to the member but as to the institute they were conditional (8). This dismissal required no special formality, except that the cause really existed and was just, whereupon the dismissal was pronounced.

This same decree (9) permitted Superiors General with their Counsel to sub-delegate members of the same religious Order or Congregation in extraordinary cases to dismiss members of the same Religion.

a) In diocesan Institutes, the dismissal of members, having professed either temporal or perpetual vows, pertained to the Ordinary of the diocese in which they resided. (10). Care had to be taken in these dismissals, so that the right of a third party

4. Decree "Auctis admodum" Nov. 4, 1892, n. 6.

5. ibid. n. 7.

6. Wernz, III, n. 676.

7. "Sacra Congregatio" n. 11; Apostolicae Sedis Oct. 12, 1869, #4; "Auctis adm." n. 9. "Quum singulae" May 16, 1911, n. 20.

8. "Sanctissimus" Jun. 12, 1858, n. 2.

9. ibid.

10. "Conditae" Dec. 8, 1900, I, n. 8; Resp. S. Congr. EE. & RR. Apr. 21, 1903.

was not injured i. e., the Ordinary could not proceed without the knowledge of the Superiors and if they justly dissented. The temporal and perpetual vows were thereby dispensed, except the vow of perpetual chastity (11).

b) In Institutes of papal approval, members could be dismissed by the Superiors General upon grave and just causes connected with incorrigibility. The sentence had effect only after it was approved by the Holy See (12). The vows, however, were dispensed by the Holy See upon a special application. (13).

Nuns, of simple or solemn vows in religious Orders so called, were dismissed for causes of like nature, if there were no hope of ammendment after a probation and there was danger of grave harm to the monastery on account of the continued faults. The opinion or decision of the Abbess or Superioress together with her Counsel was required to be given by a secret ballot (14). The matter had to be referred to the Sacred Congregation of Religious which gave further instructions for the procedure. Expulsion or dismissal had effect only after this Sacred Congregation confirmed the sentence (15).

The New Code retains much of the legislation of the Old Law, however, the changes and the division that it presents offer great aid to those who are concerned in this matter. The classification of religious into three categories presents the law in a vivid schema. In the first place, the distinction that was held in the Old Law in regard to the term "dismissal" is no more in vogue.

The dismissal of religious is treated in the New Code under a separate Title. (16). In the beginning of this Title, three instances are enumerated when a religious of whatever Order, Congregation or Institute may be considered dismissed if he or she is guilty of the crimes the law mentions. These are: a) Public apostacy from the Catholic Faith (17). By an apostate is understood, one who had entirely withdrawn from the Catholic Faith (18). This act of with-drawing or forsaking religion

12. "Conditae" II, n. 1.
13. "Conditae" II, n. 2.
14. "Quum singulae", n. 21.
15. "Quum singulae", ibid.
16. Liber II, Tit. XVI, can. 646.
17. can. 646 #1, n. 1.
18. Noldin, De Poenis Eccl. (Denp., Pustet, 1921) n. 57.

must be externally manifested (19) and public i. e. known to others or in such circumstances that it will be inevitably spread abroad (20). The withdrawl from the Catholic Faith does not necessarily include the act of embracing another religious sect as some formerly held (21), but, an act contrary to the essence of our Faith constitutes such an offense, e. g. public denial of Christian revelation would constitute an act of apostacy (22). b) A religious of either sex having pronounced either temporal or perpetual vows, that are either simple or solemn, deserting a religious institute with a person of the opposite sex is subject to immediate dismissal. The law makes here no distinction as to the person with whom the flight is taken, thus it does not lessen the gravity of the offense, it the person is not qualified to contract a marriage on account of some impediment. Likewise, the intention to marry need not be present (23) in any of the parties, wherefore, the law sets aside all doubts that may arise from these circumstances. c) Finally, those religious who contract or attempt to contract matrimony, even civilly, are guilty of an act whereby they are considered to be dismissed (24). One having profesed simple vows, by contracting a marriage does so validly, though illicitly. An attempted marriage takes place when a religious, bound by solemn vows (25) or by simple vows which by special legislation import invalidity or simply professed but in major Orders (26) tries to contract marriage. These instances of solemn or simple by special legislation and major Orders are diriment impediments to valid matrimony. An attempted marriage before a civil magistrate, although invalid on account of clandestinity, even if there were no diriment impediment on the part of the religious, is an offense punished with the same penalty of dismissal.

This dismissal of religious, who have been guilty of any one of the three offenses i. e. apostacy, flight with a person of the opposite sex and contracting or attempting marriage, comes not

19. can. 2197 n. 1.
20. Polm. Par. II, II, n. 97.
21. Noldin, 1. c.
22. can. 646, #1, n. 2.
23. Augustine, III, p. 386.
24. can. 646 #1, n. 3.
25. can. 1073.
26. can. 1072.

into effect until the major Superior i. e. the Abbot, Superior General or Provincial, together with the Chapter or Counsel declares that the act had been committed. This declaration is necessary for the validity of the dismissal (27).

The cooperation of the Chapter or Counsel with the major Superior in this dismissal is to be in accordance with the regulations which the statutes or constitutions prescribe (28). If the vote of these bodies is consultive then the Superior needs only their counsel, although, he might not abide by it; if, however, the vote is decisive then the Superior must act according to the result of the majority of the ballot.

The final act, to which the Code cautions, is to collect all proofs in relation with the matter and have them preserved in the archives of the Order or Congregation (29).

Besides the cases enumerated when a religious is dismissed ipso facto, the Old Law contained another viz., apostacy from a religious Order or Institute, if the religious did not return within three months (30). The Code has eliminated this offense from the list of ipso facto dismissals, but places it in another category. The law now binds any religious who may have apostatized from a religious Order or Institute to return to the same, and emphasizes the fact that all the obligations, which he or she may have contracted by profession, are always binding (30) even though living outside of religion. Moreover, such a religious incurs an excommunication ipso facto reserved to the major Superior or the Ordinary if the Institute is not exempt (31).

After the introduction of this title in which the ipso facto dismissal ofenses are enumerated, the Code contains the three main divisions of dismissing religious. The first concerns itself with religious of temporal vows whether exempt or not, the subsequent two contain the exempt and non-exempt perpetually or solemnly professed of all Orders or Congregations.

As to the first, religious, who pronounced temporal vows in Orders or Congregations of papal approval, may be dismissed by the Supreme Moderator i. e. the Superior General, Abbot in

27. Fanfani, De Iure Relig. n. 391.
28. Fanfani, De Iure Relig. n. 391.
29. can. 646 #2.
30. can. 645.
31. can. 2385.

autonomous monasteries with the consent of the Counsel, which is given by secret balot. The Counsel has a decisive vote in this matter (32), so that if the Superior General does not act upon the vote of this body the dismissal is invalid.

Nuns or Sisters are subject in this matter to the Ordinary of the diocese in which the religious house is situated. If they are subject to a Regular Prelate then he also has the right to dismiss them (33). There arises a difficulty in this matter when these religious are also subject to a Regular Superior i. e., whether he alone has the power, by virtue of the law in the Code, to dismiss the religious or whether he must exercise this power jointly with the Ordinary of the diocese. Blat (34) and Fanfani (35) are of the opinion that the Regular Superior must act with the Ordinary. The latter adduces for this argument other canons where the two superiors act conjointly. The law, however, states in these canons that the two must act together, while in our case of dismissal this does not seem to be conveyed in the meaning of the law. It merely states that the Regular Superior is competent to dismiss the sister or nun, if these religious are subject to him. Prummer upholds the opposite view that the Regular Superior himself has power to dismiss the religious. He gives a reason for his opinion, stating that the cumulative power of the two superiors would give rise to serious difficulties if they disagree in the matter (36). He also adds that if one considers the wording of the law as it reads in the canon, one must admit that the Regular Superior alone has the power to dismiss the religious. This latter opinion seems to be the more probable, for if the Code desired that the two superiors should act jointly in the matter then it would have used more definite terms indicating this intention. The wording of the canon reads independently, so that the Ordinary or Superior may perform the act. Vermeersh cautions that, although the grammatical construction seems to imply this meaning, nevertheless, it is to be considered as improbable, and in the meantime to follow the safer opinion i. e. that the two su-

32. Prummer, Manuale Iuris Eccles. n. 258.
33. can. 647 #1.
34. De Personis II, n. 729.
35. De Iure Relig. n. 395.
36. Prummer, Manuale Iuris Eccl. n. 258 note.

periors should act together until this question will be defined by an authentic declaration (37).

In diocesan Institutes the Ordinary of the diocese, in which the religious house is situated, has the faculty to dismiss members, however, should not use this power without the knowledge or contrary to the will of the Superiors or Superioresses, especially if they have a just reason for dissenting, because this would harm the acquired right of a third party.

The cause for dismissal must be grave (38). It may arise either from the member or the religious community. A want of religious spirit that causes scandal to the community is a sufficient cause for dismissal, if the following conditions were observed viz., that the member had been admonished repeatedly, at least twice we think is sufficient (39), provided that some time is allowed in the interim for amendment, which is left to the prudent judgment of the superior, and together with the admonition some penance was imposed by the superior upon the member.

The admonition should be of such a nature as to present a proof of the fact that it had been given. It would be sufficient, if it is given before one witness or even two which answers to all requirements of law in our instance. A written note of the fact should be kept for future eventualities.

The penance, that is imposed. should be prompted by prudent judgment so that the desired effect could be hoped for more readily unless a too severe one might be rather to the detriment of the individual. If the member continues in the ill-will even after the second admonition, then the Superior or Superioress may proceed with the dismissal according to the prescribed rules. The Causes ,for which the dismissal is made, must be known with certainty to the one that does the dismissing. In diocesan Institutes the whole matter should be referred to the Ordinary. Ill health is not a cause for dismissing one. if it were contracted after the entrance to the community or if the member being in such condition informed beforehand the authorities of the fact who received the person into religion. A member may be dismissed for ill health, if this fact was wilfully concealed in order

37. Vermeersch, Epitome Iuris Can. I, n. 653, p. 329.
38. can. 647 #2 n. 1.
39. can. 660.

to deceive the authorities (40). The entrance, thus gained into the community, is unlawful for thereby harm arises to the community against which it has a right to protect itself.

Previous to taking any steps in this matter to dismiss a religious, the Superior should have such proofs in his possession that will convince prudent men. The procedure here does not require any judicial formalities (41). The Superior, who pronounces the dismissal, must manifest to the religious the causes for which he or she is being dismissed in order that the religious may present a defense. If a Superior dismisses a religious who has presented a defense in the case and the latter thinks that the act was not just, he has a remedy at his disposal in the form of a recourse to the Holy See i. e. the Sacred Congregation of Religious; pending the recourse the decree of dismissal has no effect (42).

The effects of a dismissal are: a) the religious is thereby freed from the obligations of the vows, except those that arise from major Orders if he had been elevated to these, besides such a one must return to his diocese and the Ordinary has a duty to receive him (43). If the religious is a cleric in minor Orders, these automatically cease, and he is reduced to the lay state (44).

The second division includes all religious who pronounced perpetual vows either in a clerical Institute, though not exempt, or in a lay religion. First to be considered are those Congregations of men which are either strictly clerical, though not exempt, or those religious Congregations and Institutes which have nonclerical members i. e. lay religious, who pronounce perpetual vows whether simple or solemn and are not exempt (45).

Certain conditions must be observed previous to any proceedings for dismissal. Just as grave causes are necessary for dismissing a religious of temporal profession, so there must exist not only grave causes but real violations of law, for which a member of a community is dismissed. Three violations are

40. can. 647 #2, n. 2
41. can. 647 #2 n. 3
42. can. 647 #2 n. 4
43. can. 641 #1.
44. can. 648.
45. Fanfani, 1. c. n. 398.

necessary for dismissal (46). These may be of the same (47) or different species, so that when taken together, they clearly manifest a perverse will of the religious and his determination to remain obstinate (48). One violation may, even, be sufficient for dismissal, if it is permanent i. e. having been committed three different times after canonical admonitions preceded (49). The violations, by which the common law or a special law of the religious is transgressed or violated, must not only be grave but external. This point will be considered more fully later on when treating of procedure proper.

The admonitions, that are given to the delinquent by the Superior, may only follow, when there is a certainty that a violation of a law had been committed (50). The Superior, who gives the admonition, is the immediate major Superior of the house or, if the Congregation is divided into provinces, then the Provincial or whom the constitutions or statutes may designate to be the Superior. The admonitions are given orally before two witnesses or in the presence of a notary, who is a member of the community that is chosen and appointed for this purpose by the Superior. These admonitions are to be noted in writing and preserved in the register of the religious Congregation or Institute. The admonitions may be intimated in writing to the failing religious. The dispatching of the written instrument, containing the admonition, should be sent in a manner which guarantees the receipt of it, i. e. by registered mail.

The third condition is the evident defect of ammendment on the part of the religious who had committed the violations. This is considered to exist when the religious, after having been admonished twice, does not reform his manner of action by abstaining from committing other violations. A third commission is considered to demonstrate this state of mind (51).

The mode of proceeding in dismissing these religious of per-

---

46. can. 649.
47. can. 657
48. can. 649 & 657.
49. can. 657.
50. can. 658.
51. can. 662.

petual vows is as follows: when the three conditions enumerated above viz., the existence of grave external violations, two admonitions and want of amendment are found to exist from definite evidence collected or received by the major Superior, thereupon, he should carefuly consider the matter with his Counsel and decide whether there is sufficient ground to proceed further in the matter. This decision is made by a ballot. If the majority of the votes is for the dismissal (52), then action is taken to dismiss the religious.

If the religious is of a diocesan Institute, the whole matter is referred to the Ordinary of the place where the religious house is situated, who, according to his prudent judgment, may pronounce the dismissal. The Ordinary must observe the same rules as those regulating the dismissal of religious temporally professed, viz., that the matter is a serious importance, wherefore, there must be sufficient grave causes for the action.

It is not sufficient that the one who pronounces the dismissal is personally convinced of the sufficiency of the facts, but, the proofs must be of such a nature that they would stand the test if produced before an ecclesiastical tribunal.

The Ordinary must inform the member of these causes and grant him sufficient time to present his defense. After having well considered the proofs and defense, the Ordinary may decree a dismissal. Against this decision, the religious has a right of recourse to the Holy See i. e. to the Sacred Congregation of Religious.

If the religious, to be dismissed, is a member of a Congregation or Institute of papal approval, the Supreme Moderator, who is the General or such Superior that governs the whole religious Congregation, has the power to give the decree of dismissal. It has no effect, unless, it is confirmed by the Holy See (53). As in the former case, so also here the religious has a right to present a defense to the Superior General. The evidence and the defense are to be carefully recorded in order that, in case of a recourse, the whole matter may be sent to the Sacred Congregation.

52. can. 650 #2.
53. can. 650 #2, n. 2.

We come now to the consideration of Orders, Congregations and Institutes of women of diocesan or papal approval in which simple perpetual or solemn vows are professed. The causes for dismissal are grave, external (54) i. e. such as are known to the community (55) and are incorrigible.

The religious who has committed some serious fault should be admonished. The admonitions are not canonical for the Code makes no mention of them, however, we think that these are given in some form by the Superioress, especially, since the law requires (56) that sufficient time be given for a probation. This, no doubt, implies some effort on the part of those who have charge of the Institute; furthermore, in order to decide that one is incorrigible there must be evidence of such a state of mind and this is best demonstrated through admonition.

Proceedings for dismissal are taken when the religious gives no hope of amendment. In diocesan Institutes, the whole matter must be sent to the local Ordinary who, after careful consideration, will make his decision according to the facts presented.

If the Congregation is of papal approval, the Superioress General (57) collects all the matter and transmits it to the Sacred Congregation of Religious.

In case of nuns, the Ordinary, in whose diocese the convent is situated, collects all proceedings and documents which he forwords to the Sacred Congregation together with his own decision upon the matter and, if the Order is subject to Regulars, also with the decision given by the Regular Prelate (58). All the religious have a right to present their own defense in case of dismissal (59). These pleas, as they may be called, must be recorded in the proceedings.

The religious, who is dismissed by the Sacred Congregation or the Ordinary, must not be permitted to leave the community without sufficient sustenance in order to return home or to reach

---

54. can. 651 #1; "Quum singulae", n. 21.
55. Blat, 1. c. n. 734, p. 725.
56. can. 651 #1.
57. can. 652 #3.
58. can. 652 #2.
59. can. 651 #2.

such other place where she makes her habitation. The dowry that she may have brought to the Institute when she entered, must be returned to her (60); if there were no dowry required, the community, from which she is dismissed, must provide her with support at its own expense, which must be done out of charity (61). The Ordinary or the Congregation will decide what amount is to be given and for how long a time. If the community is unwilling and refuses to do so, the Ordinary has power by common law to compel it to give this support (62).

Finally, the law contains a special provision for dismissals in extraordinary cases. These are: a) a grave and public scandal, b) a very grave and imminent harm which is about to befall a community. The crime must be publicly known outside of the religious community or in such circumstances that it will certainly become known, in consequence of which grave scandal will arise among the faithful. Scandal, here, is considered by law to be a grave cause for it is to the detriment of the faithful and the religious community, if the author of a notorious crime is not dismissed.

The other cause, an imminent and very grave harm that is about to befall a community, is sufficient for immediate dismissal. The harm must be actually threatening, not a mere danger that is remote or uncertain (63). There must be a moral certainty as to its real existence. The harm may menace the whole community or an individual of it e. g. a threat to destroy the property or the life of any member.

The formality required in these extreme cases is, that the major Superior or, if he cannot be reached in due time then, the local Superior with the Counsel or Chapter having considered the matter, will pronounce the dismissal. When the local Superior with the Counsel act to dismiss a religious, the consent of the local Ordinary is necessary (64). This is the case with Institutes of papal approval; for in diocesan communities the Ordinary is the Superior who has full power to make the dismissal.

60. can. 551 #1.
61. can. 643 #4.
62. can. ibid.
63. Vermeersch, 1. c. n. 658, p. 332.
64. can. 653.

The whole matter is immediately sent by the major Superior or the Ordinary to the Sacred Congregation of Religious in order to obtain a confirmation of the dismissal.

The effect of this dismissal is that the religious at once sets aside the habit with which he had been invested and leaves the community.

This dismissal is applied to all religious men and women, for it is a general law (65).

65. can. 490.

CRIME OR VIOLATION OF LAW

We have seen that for a dismissal of religious with temporal profession and those of perpetual profession in Institutes of women grave causes are required (1), while, for dismissal of religious men who pronounced perpetual vows in clerical Institutes, though not exempt, and of lay religious whether exempt or not (2), grave causes are not only necessary, but, there must be external violations of a law (3). The dismissal of non-exempt religious whether clerical or lay differs from that of the clerical exempt Orders or Congregations in the mode of procedure, but, the causes required for both categories are of the same nature.

These causes are termed crimes or violations of law or "delictum" as the Code contains. There are other terms used in the New Law to designate grave actions by which a law is violated such are, "crimen" (4) and "transgressio" (5), however, the Code retains the term "delictum" throughout its penal section (6), and in other parts of it we find this same term used when there is mention of grave violations of law. These various terms do not convey a distinction such as is found in our modern civil codices. There was no such distinction found in the old sources of ecclesiastical law nor is it introduced into the New Law (7). The Code uses only the one term "delictum" throughout the penal section with the one exception above i. e. crime. The term crime or violation will be used in this theme to designate the Latin word "delictum" and the meaning of it will be that which the Code defines it to have in its penal section. By crime is understood an external and morally imputable violation of a law to which a penalty is attached at least in an undetermined manner (8). It is an act whereby the social order of a society is gravely disturbed (9). In the Church also which is a perfect society such disturbances may and do happen; wherefore, she has taken precautions from time immemorial to prevent them.

1. can. 647 #2 n. 1; can. 651 #1.
2. Fanfani, l. c. n. 398.
3. can. 649. & 656 n. 1.
4. Lib. V, tit. XV "De crimine falsi"; can. 2363; can. 1042 #2, n. 5.
5. can. 2222.
6. Lib. V.
7. Chelodi, Jus poenale, n. 3.
8. can. 2195 #1.
9. Wernz, Jus penale eccl. VI, n. 13.

Among the constitutive elements of crime we find the first to be its external character. The violation of a law consists in an external act. This act must be such that can be perceived through the senses (10) e. g. to strike a prelate. The Church does not judge internal acts in her external forum. As St. Thomas says: "De iis potest homo legem facere, de quibus potest iudicare. Iudicium autem hominis esse non potest de interioribus actibus qui latent, sed solum de exterioribus motibus qui apparent" (11).

The coercive power, that the Church possesses, is directed for the purpose of maintaining and preserving social order. Not all external grave commissions are subject to ecclesiastical punishments, but, only those which, according to prudent judgment of competent legislators, are injurious to society (12). It may be summed up, that all those crimes, enumerated in the penal part of the Code to which a penalty is attached whether it be determined or not, are expressly designated to disturb social order, and, therefore, are real crimes in the sense of the law.

Crime is divided into three classes by reason of the knowledge that may or may not be had of it. The various divisions, into which crime was classed by authors previous to the New Law, are now abandoned. Only those which the Code enumerates are of practical importance to the judge or superior.

Crime is either public or occult. A public crime is one that is already divulged or happens to be in such circumstances, according to the prudent judgment of men, that it will easily be made known (13). This imports knowledge of the fact by others besides the author of the crime. It may be already known or on the verge of being brought to the attention of others. A crime, that is known by only a few, e. g. three or in a large community e. g. a city by even more who will neither divulge the knowledge of such a violation of law nor give any proofs of it, cannot be considered public; for that must be considered as occult what only a few, but, prudent men know, because it is as though no one knew it (14). On the other hand, if there is a number

10. Sabetti-Barrett, Theol. Moral. n. 2, p. 10.
11. Ia IIae. q. 91, a. 4; Caviglioli, De censuris, n. 35.
12. Wernz, 1. c. n. 13.
13. can. 2197, n. 1.
14. D'Annibale, Summa Theol. Moral I, parg. 242, not. 49.

of those who have knowledge of a fact, even though in a large community, it may be presumed that the report of it will, without doubt, be spread among others in no long space of time. The character and qualities of persons who are aware of a crime must be taken into consideration just as their number; for ability to spread a sensational report is, even, considered an accomplishment by not a few.

A public crime may be notorious. By notoriety is understood something well known or universally recognized. The evidence is so certain that it cannot be concealed or disproved. A notorious crime is a species of public crime. Notoriety is of fact and of law.

Notoriety of fact implies that a crime is publicly known to the extent that it can neither be concealed nor condoned by law (15). The factors that are taken into consideration with notoriety are time, place and multitude of persons that witness the fact.

Time was regarded important by older canonists. Thus daytime was considered to be necessary for notoriety, although, a crime committed during night could become notorious, if there were a sufficient number of persons present to warrant the spreading of the fact among the rest of the neighbors (16). The place, in which the crime had been committed, had to be connected with a community in order that the people, could be fully aware of it (17). The multitude or rather the number of persons, that was necessary for a crime to become notorious, was an open question of opinion among authors. Some asserted that the whole locality e. g. city had to know of the fact; others that a majority sufficed, while, another group held that a limited number of ten was sufficient and finally, the extremists maintained that three were enough (18). Canonists, however, agreed that the best judge of this fact was the tribunal to whom the case was referred (19), for where the law did not expressly state or decide, it was for the judge to determine.

Having considered the factors that constitute a violation as

15. can. 2197, n. 3.
16. Schmalz. V. 1, n. 5.
17. ibid. n. 4.
18. ibid. n. 6.
19. ibid. n. 6.

notorious, we may observe that notoriety of a crime consists not only in the knowledge of the fact, but, in the knowledge of the same as something positively criminal; e. g. a murder is notorious (20) when a person is publicly known to have taken another's life unlawfully. If, it were a mere homicide committed in self-defense, then, it could not be termed notorious on account of the act itself, because there is no evil or unjust intention through which it was done. It is an act of self-protection to which everyone has a natural right.

Notoriety of law is that notoriety which the law expressly attaches to certain cases. It is established either through a confession in court or by becoming an adjudicated case, "res judicata". Notoriety by confession is when the author confesses a crime either spontaneously before a tribunal or in answer to the questioning of a judge acknowledges it and does not immediately recant it (21). It may be done orally or by written instrument which contains the confession; wherefor, a crime becomes an established fact of notoriety. Notoriety by a sentence means when two different tribunals, to whom the case had been brought, have given two conforming decisions (22). In like manner, if only one sentence had been given, but no appeal had been made within the prescribed time (23). In both cases the crime becomes an established fact and publicly known in consequence of which it is notorious by law.

A crime is occult when it is not public (24) i. e. when it is not divulged or there is no danger that it will be. A crime known to a few persons, two or three, who may be trusted not to tell it to others, may be considered occult. On the other hand, a crime known to a few only, e. g. four or six in a large community, but destined in a short time to be divulged to many may be considered public.

An occult crime may be occult materially or formally. The former denotes that the crime is not known i. e. the criminal act itself is unknown e. g. to pronounce a heresy alone in one's private room is a crime that is occult materially. It is an external

20. Wernz, VI, n. 17.
21. can. 1750.
22. can. 1902, n. 1.
23. can. 1902, n. 2.
24. can. 2197, n. 4.

and morally imputable act by which the ecclesiastical law is violated, but on account of the circumstances it is hidden from others. This does not excuse the author of the heresy from punishment which the Code contains and that is incurred ipso facto (25).

By a formally occult crime is meant that the crime itself is known, but the imputability is unknown (26) e. g., if one be found slain, but the slayer is unknown. This may also be the case when the fact itself is known to others and the author is identified with the crime, provided that the motive, through which it was committed, is misconceived or excuses him from imputability (27), e. g., if both the homicide and the slayer are known, but the act has the appearence of being done in self-defense, the crime remains formally occult. Furthermore, a case may be formally occult even after having been brought to a tribunal, if it should have been dismissed, at least, before the pleading, although it were done through unjust or false testimony (28). The reason for this is that the defendant had not been proven guilty of a charge which had been made against him. Finally a crime is entirely occult if it cannot be proven in court (29).

The second constitutive element of crime is its moral imputability. To impute something to someone signifies to attribute or refer the act or thing to a person as the moral cause i. e. the fully conscious and willing agent (30). Imputability is subjective being in the cause from which an act emanates i. e. coming from man a moral being who performs acts that are either worthy of praise or blame. These acts are human because they proceed from a free will which is the foundation of imputability (31).

The subjective elements of crime are contained in a full knowledge on the part of the intellect and freedom on the part of the will; without these there cannot be an intention to

25. can. 2314.
26. can. 2197, n. 4.
27. Sole, De delictis et poenis, n. 10.
28. Lega, III, n. 131, note 1 and n. 244; Sole, 1. c. n. 10.
29. Wernz, VI, n. 17.
30. Sole, 1. c. n. 3.
31. Sabetti-Barrett, Theol. Moral. n. 1, p.

commit a crime, which forms the basis of imputability (32). Imputability is determined according to the knowledge and deliberation with which one commits a crime. When the intellect and the will are prevented from functioning as they should, the responsibility is lessened in proportion to the defect that arises in these faculties on account of the existing impediments. A crime cannot be committed, unless the delinquent had an intention to violate a law; when such an intention is made knowingly and deliberately, it is known as malice (33). This intention or resolve to violate a law cannot be conceived without liberty of action and knowledge of the law or, at least, of the harm that will result from such violation; wherefore, anything that might prevent the intellect from attaining the proper knowledge and the will from exercising its free acts, also affects the malice and makes it less imputable or even takes away all imputability (34).

There are many causes that impede, either partially or wholly, the operations of the intellect and the will, the very roots of a moral act. Positive law, based upon natural law, designates these causes for mutual benefit of the governing and the governed. The necessity of this is evident, especially, in those instances where natural law is not definitely stated, or where positive law requires more than natural law, or determines certain general rules, as presumptions of law e. g. certain age or sex.

The conditions that effect imputability on the part of the intellect are:

a) want of the use of reason (35). Knowledge is an essential requisite for a moral act, if this is lacking then, there can be no human act and consequently, there is no responsibility.

b) Age, also, is a factor which either excuses from all imputability or diminishes it. Persons who have completed the twenty first year are known as majors, all under this age are minors. Boys who have completed the age of fourteen and girls the twelfth year are pubescent. All under the age of seven are infants (36). Infants are excused from all legal imputability, because not having the use of reason they are incapable of malice

32. Werns, VI, n. 19.
33. can. 2200; Wernz, VI, n. 20; Lega, III, n. 23.
34. Lega, III, n. 26.
35. can. 2201 #1.
36. can. 88.

which presupposes the use of it (37). Should there be an instance, when one under the age of seven had the use of reason, even then he would be exempt as the law now provides for such cases (38). Minor age diminishes imputability, unless otherwise provided in the law; this diminution becomes greater as it nears the age of infancy (39). Those, under the age of puberty, are exempted from incurring penalties ipso facto (40), likewise, they should not be punished with vindicative punishments (41), but, only with corrective punishments that best befit their age. Those that have passed the age of puberty may be punished according to the penalties prescribed in the law (42).

In criminal matters, the age of puberty, in the Old Law, was considered to be the fourteenth year for both sexes (43), because the law, in this instance, received wider interpretation; this may, even, be probable today, although, the ages of twelve and fourteen respectively are according to the letter of the law.

c) Passion is a movement of the sensitive appetite which affects the will by intensifying its act and beclouds the intellect so that it is incapable of proper functioning (44) and thus, it renders an act less voluntary and in consequence less imputable (45). Involuntary passion arises suddenly and unexpectedly; it is an obstacle to deliberation and diminishes imputability in various degrees according to the violence of the attack and the incapability of the agent's resistance (46). Should the impetus of passion be so great that it would make deliberation impossible and completely impede the consent of the will, then the person, under said conditions, would be free from all imputability (47). Voluntary pasion, that is deliberately excited and sustained, increases the guilt of an agent because he acts with malice which deserves to be punished in accordance to its gravity. In the

37. can. 88 #3; V, 5, c. 1 in Clem; Schmalz., V, 23, n. 4, 5; Lega, III, n. 28.
38. can. 12.
39. can. 2204.
40. can. 2230.
41. can. 2230.
42. can. 2230.
43. Lega, III, n. 28.
44. Wernz, VI, n. 36.
45. can. 2206.
46. Arynhac, n. 17. p. 39.
47. can. 2206.

external forum, imputability is always presumed in a delinquent and only a proof to the contrary will free him from any culpability.

d) Violence is an application of force under which one is compelled to act contrary to his will. Actions, which are placed under constraint that cannot be resisted, are not the result of a malicious intention and, consequently, are not imputable (48). Should one fall a victim to violence through his own fault or negligence and in this condition commit a violation of a law, he is guilty of the action, however, the imputability is diminished on account of the existing circumstance. If violence prevents all freedom of action, then a violation of a law committed under such circumstances cannot be imputed to be a crime (49). Fear is a perturbation of the mind on account of a future impending danger (50). It influences the will to choose that which otherwise it would not have selected. Yet, an act, placed under the constraint of grave fear, is voluntary because the power of deliberation is still retained and only the exercise of the faculties is impeded (51).

Fear is absolute or relative. Absolute fear is grave in itself i. e. in its own nature: it is known to be such, when it perturbs the mind of a steadfast man (52). This disturbance of the mind through fear must be such that prudent and firm men, when affected by it, are unable to be masters of their deliberations (53). Relative fear is not grave in itself, however, on account of the personal disposition of an individual that is influenced, it may become such when a grave perturbation of the mind results from it. Hence, in determining the imputability of a violation of law, not only must the nature of a harmful threat be taken into consideration, but, also the person that suffers under it.

Grave or relative fear, in case of necessity or a serious disadvantage as i rule, excuses from observing ecclesiastical law (54). Ecclesiastical laws, as all human laws, generally do not oblige one under grave inconvenience. Grave fear does not

48. C. 5, X, I, 40.
49. can. 2205 #1.
50. Polm. n. 178, p. 137.
51. Sole. 1. c., n. 33.
52. C. 4, X, I, 40.
53. ibid.
54. can. 2205 #2.

excuse from crime, but, only diminishes the degree of imputability when an act is intrinsically evil or in contempt of religion, ecclesiastical authority or to the detriment of the salvation of souls (55).

e) Ignorance is want of knowledge in one capable of receiving it (56). Ignorance of fact excuses from imputability, if it is invincible i. e. without fault, for the ancient rule "Ignorantia facti non iuris excusat" (57) clearly demonstrates this principle. It might seem that ignorance of law, according to this rule, would not excuse, however, it must be understood that this has reference to external forum (58), where ignorance of law is not presumed, unless, it is proven. Ignorance of law, if it is not culpable, excuses from all imputability (59); whilst, culpable ignorance of law or fact does not excuse from imputability, but, lessens it according to the degree of negligence that existed (60). Ignorance of penalty does not excuse from a crime, although, it somewhat diminished imputability (61). What has been stated concerning ignorance may in like manner be applied to inadvertance and error (62).

f) Crime is not only imputable to a delinquent on account of malice through which it was committed, but, also on account of culpable negligence (63). A violation of a law through malice proceeds from a wilful and intended resolve to do wrong, whilst, a violation through negligence or fault is an omission of proper attention or deliberation that does not imply a direct intention to violate a law, but, the action, thus placed is imputable to the author who could have and should have forseen the harm that results from it (64).

If a law is violated through culpable negligence, imputability is diminished in proportion to the culpability of a delinquent which is determined by the superior or judge from existing cir-

55. can. 2205 #3.
56. Polm. n. 198, p. 143.
57. Reg. Iuris n. 13 in VI.
58. Arynhac, 1. c. n. 12, p. 34.
59. can. 2202 #1.
60. ibid.
61. can. 2202 #2.
62. can. 2202 #3.
63. can. 2199.
64. Wernz, VI, n. 23.

cumstances (65). Such a violation is not a crime in the strict sense of the term, for it is not committed with full deliberation which is always necessary for a crime.

A casual happening is free from all imputability. The harm that is caused through an accident cannot be forseen; it is not done through malice of fore-thought and, consequently, is not culpable (66).

The third element of crime is the violation of a law. Members of a society are obliged to observe the laws that are laid down for that body, otherwise, they will be guilty of transgression. An external violation of laws of a society e. g. Church, disturbs social order. It constitutes a crime for which punishment is demanded in the interest of general good (67). Not every transgression of a law is a crime, but only that violation which injures social order in consequence of which harm arises to a society. Any other trangression of a law that does not cause a disturbance of social order is not a crime.

Considering crime in itself, the essential element of it is the injury that it inflicts upon society and this is the object of a penalty. Ecclesiastical legislation has attached penalties, either determined or undetermined, to those violations of law that disturb social order, in order to indicate those acts as real crimes. This does not prevent an ecclesiastical superior from punishing those transgressions of law that are not contained among the liable acts of the penal section of the Code, if scandal or gravity of transgression should demand it (68); otherwise, if the attachment of a penalty were required, a delinquent could not be punished without first having been admonished to that effect.

In civil legislation only such violations are considered crimes as are indicated by law, hence, the adage "Nullum crimen sine lege". This is for the reason that the threefold power i. e. legislative, judicial and executive, is not vested in one person, as is the case in the Church. On this account, the power of civil authorities is limited. A superior in the Church, who has jurisdiction, possesses full legislative, judicial and executive power, consequently, he may declare even such transgressions as are

65. can. 2203 #1.
66. can. 2203 #2.
67. Wernz, VI, n. 14.
68. can. 2222 #1.

not expressly contained in ecclesiastical law to be causes of disturbing social order and may attach certain penalties to the same (69).

Superiors, having full power, may not only declare certain transgressions to be grave disturbances of social order and punish them, but, they may impose precepts upon their subjects, obliging them to abide by such commands. If a penalty is attached to a precept ,it has the same effect as an ecclesiastical penal law, i. e. the transgression of it will constitute a crime in the juridical meaning (70). Moreover, superiors may attach penalties not only to laws which they have legislated, but also to all other whether divine or ecclesiastical, as long as these are binding in their territory, and so long as circumstances or conditions require such measures (71).

There is a distinction between a transgression of a law and a violation of one. The former is an offense against a law which has no penalty, while the latter is a more grave act by which social order is disturbed and to which a penalty is attached. Again crime is distinguished from sin; both are equal in that they are morally evil on account of the voluntary violation of a law; however, they differ in external effects. Sin is a transgression of a law that may be done by a mere internal act of the will, thereby social order is not injured; consequently, no penalty from a human authority is incurred. By crime a law is violated externally so that grave harm is done to social order. The act is not only imputable in consience, but, the violator is guilty in the external forum and may be punished by penalties established by law for the sake of restoring impaired social order (72). Keeping this distinction in mind, there is no difficulty to understand the principle of ecclesiastical public legislation viz.: "Ecclesia non iudicat de occultis" (73). The Church does not judge internal matters of conscience, in as far as she is an external society, because as such she has an external forum in which only that is judged what can be perceived.

---

69. Suarez, De lege, Lib. V, c. 11; Wernz, VI, n. 14; Lega, III, n, 16; Cavagnis, Institutiones, I, n. 138.

70. can. 2195 #2.

71. can. 2221.

72. Wernz VI, n. 14; Lega, III, n. 48; Sole, 1. c. n. 5.

73. Sole, 1. c. n. 5.

EXTRAJUDICIAL INQUIRY

By inquiry is understood an investigation, a searching into or an examination for the purpose of obtaining authentic information concerning some definite thing. Not every investigation or searching into is an inquiry as understood here, but, only that investigation which is made for discovering or detecting a crime or the author thereof. In a juridical sense, inquiry means an investigation legally conducted by a judge or superior in order to discover a crime and its author (1).

Inquiry is divided into general and special (2). By general inquiry is meant an investigation conducted by an ecclesiastical judge or superior, merely in virtue of his office, not prompted by any particular transgression. Thus an Ordinary in his diocese or a religious Superior in his province or monastery, during a visitation, inquires whether the laws and statutes are observed, if there exist any violations or trangressions or, if there might be reports of any such offenses.

Special inquiry is an investigation of a violation of a law, conducted by a competent ecclesiastical judge or Superior in virtue of his office. Special inquiry is divided into extrajudicial and judicial.

Extrajudicial inquiry is used outside of a procedure, as the term itself suggests, in order to obtain evidence of the existence

1. Schmalzgrueber, V, tit. I, n. 172: Reiff. h. t. n. 149; Pirhing, h. t. n. 47; Wernz, V, n. 842, p. 76; Schmier, V, tr, I, n. 61; Bouix, De iudiciis, vol. II, p. 60.

2. Reiff. 1. c. n. 150; Schmier, 1. c. n. 66; Wernz, 1. c. n. 843, p. 77. Some authors divided inquiry into general, special and mixed (Schmalz. 1. c. n. 174; Bouix, 1. c., p. 61); or into most general or general, general or mixed, and special as (Pirhing, 1. c., n. 48; Fagnanus, Commentarium, V, De Accusatione, c. Qualiter, n. 40); or general, special and most special as (Lega, vol. IV, n. 141, p. 201). The general or most general was the inquiry conducted in visitations or synods i. e. where there was no previous cause requiring it, the superior did it merely "ex mero officio"; the special was in inquiry directed to a given crime and person who was previously designated by denunciation or defamation, the judge acte "ex officio"; the mixed was when the crime was either specified and the author uncertain or vice versa. The most special, as Lega mentions, was exercised by the Promotor of justice when there was a hearing of a case, it was his duty to see that all investigations were completed against the defendant. In general the canonist agreed upon the meaning of the various inquiries, although, the terms varied according to different authors.

of a trangression or a violation of a law, previous to the application of penal remedies or penalties. It is instituted after a previous general inquiry, denunciation or a well founded rumor of a violation or a transgression. A Superior, having obtained this information, has a right and duty to make further investigation in order to determine whether his subject is guilty of the alleged misconduct or violation. No previous infamy is required for this inquiry, because it is conducted secretly (3).

If the conduct of a religious does not conform to his state of life and causes scandal, or there is grave danger of it in the near future on account of voluntary occasions to which he rashly exposes himself, the Superior's duty is to prevent that evil which is to the detriment of his subject and of the community. A Superior may obtain knowledge of misconduct of his subjects in various ways: from local Superiors, by his own observation, or through information from others. It is his duty to consider the matter prudently, and if there are grave indications, although they may seem doutbful, an inquiry may be begun (4). If a Superior has absolute knowledge of a fact of a violation, there is no need of an investigation and he may proceed in any manner that is just .

Even, if a fact is considered notorious, inquiry should not be ommitted, for it may happen that after a careful investigation the matter will prove to be less serious than at first report appears. This inquiry is conducted without any external formality in order to protect the person's reputation who is under investigation.

The persons who have any knowledge of the matter are to be examined seperately and secretly, in order that no unnecessary attention is attracted. That evidence, which pertains directly or indirectly to the fact of transgression or violation, should only be sought. The witnesses are to be questioned with proper discretion concerning the matter, first in a general way and then progressing to details. A record of the evidence should be made in writing.

The Superior must take into consideration the persons and the quality of the existing evidences and according to these

---

3. Acta S. S. vol. XV, p. 379.
4. Droste, Canonical Procedure, n. 87, p. 146.

make his conclusions. If the proofs obtained in the inquiry is not convincing, but merely gives rise to suspicion, the Superior, previous to applying a paternal admonition, will prudently inform his subject of the charges made against him, however, not revealing their source. If the subject, who is permitted to defend himself, vindicates himself and refutes the alleged charges, the matter is dismissed (5). In like manner, those, who have promised to alter their mode of action and to repair any harm that might have been done, are to be considered to have made satisfaction, if they comply with their resolution.

---

5. Acta S. S. 1. c. p. 380.

JUDICIAL INQUIRY

Judicial inquiry is that investigation which precedes a trial; it is employed to obtain a definite evidence of a public violation of a law that is necessary for an indictment (1).

This judicial inquiry always precedes a procedure (2) in trials for the dismissal of exempt religious whenever a crime is not notorious (3) or confessed extrajudicially (4).

It is conducted by the immediate major Superior (5) i. e. Abbot, Provincial, Prior etc., although, he may delegate a religious of the same Order or Congreagtion to be the auditor of this investigation. If the major Superior is at the same time the Supreme Moderator of an Order or monastic Confederation e. g. Superior General, President Abbot or Abbot General, this inquiry should be committed to someone else who is a member of the same religious body. A major Superior who, at the same time, is the supreme Moderator by virtue of this office is a judge of the collegiate tribunal that proceeds against a religious and pronounces the sentence of dismissal.

The one, who conducts an inquiry, obtains, without doubt, certain views about the matter that are favorable or unfavorable to the person under investigation. If such a person is a judge in the same case his preconceived opinion of the matter cannot but influence his judgment in the final decision. For this reason, equity demands that there should be a different person for each office i. e. the inquiry and the tribunal, in order to assure an unbiased administration of justice. It may be objected, that the law does not expressly forbid this, but, rather, permits it (6); this is true ,however, at the same time it states that as a general rule this inquiry should be conduced by some one else than the Ordinary (7) who is, at the same time, a judge of the case. In like manner, when the immediate major Superior is, at the same time, the supreme Moderator of an Order and therefore judge, he should delegate this office of inquiry to another person.

1. Wernz, V, n. 843, p. 77.
2. can. 658 #1.
3. can. 2197 n. 3.
4. can. 1753.
5. can. 1940.
6. can. 1940.
7. can. ibid.

The judge of a tribunal examines whether the admonitions had been given validly by inspecting instruments that present evidence of existing violations of law and by making sure that these acts had been executed in the proper form. If he conducted the inquiry himself and gave the admonitions then, as a judge of the tribunal, he would examine his own proceedings and in consequence, pass judgments in his own case. This is the very thing that the law tries to obviate; for this reason the auditor of inquiry should be a different person from the judge of the same case.

A special auditor of inquiry is appointed for each case (8). This office is generally considered burdensome and disagreeable, for the process of investigation is, at times, long and tedious, requiring much patience and good judgment on the part of those conducting it. The auditor of inquiry should be a religious of the same Order as the one on trial, and one known for his prudence and ability to conduct such matters. The members of the Counsel or Chapter, who form the collegiate tribunal cannot be delegated to conduct the investigation, nor those who are deputed to constitute such a tribunal in distant regions (9); for an inquisitor cannot be a judge in the same case. (10).

The auditor of inquiry being bound by the same obligations as an ordinary judge, must take an oath of office (11) to observe secrecy and to fulfill his duty faithfully. This oath is administered by the supreme Moderator (12) or his delegate in presence of a secretary (13), who records the fact in the proceedings of the inquiry. The Moderator or major Superior, if the latter conducts the inquiry himself, appoints a notary or a secretary, whose duty is to note in writing all proceedings of the inquiry in order that these may be considered authentic and have juridical value (14).

The inquiry must always be conducted secretly (15) and with great care, lest, the nature of the case be made unnecessarily pub-

8. can. 1941 #1.
9. can. 667.
10. can. 1943 #3.
11. can. 1941 #2.
12. can. 1621 #1.
13. 1621 #2.
14. can. 1585 #1 & 503.
15. can. 1943.

lic to the detriment of the religious under investigation. Should it be conducted in such a manner as to injure his good name, he has the right of defense through a recourse against such action. The law stresses prudence of action in this matter in view of the uncertain outcome of the inquiry i. e. there may not be sufficient evidence for an alleged violation or its imputability. Again secrecy is needed to avoid scandal among the community of religious and the faithful. Care must be taken not to divulge the violation through unnecessary information of the inquiry to others than those to be examined; for this reason, that number is to be limited and those persons, whose character is of such a nature that they might violate an oath of secrecy, are excluded. As the good reputation of a person must not be permitted to be called into question or to suffer harm, none are to be examined who have no knowledge of the fact nor are they, to whom the person is very well known, unless, a necessity requires it (16).

This inquiry is made in a definite order by collecting necessary proofs and then drawing them up in a final form. The object of it is to substantiate the existence of a violation and the imputability of its author. The necessity of this is evident, for no one is to be cited before a tribunal, unless, there are existing evidences of a violation (17). The basis of a crime is established through an examination of the place of its happening (18), authentic information, extrajudicial confession and testimony of witnesses (19).

In order to attain this purpose of an inquiry, the major Superior or the auditor through the authorization of the supreme Moderator will cite those, who have a knowledge of the facts relative to the case, and question them under oath to inform him of the facts and circumstances of the whole matter (20). Those to be called to give information or to testify are persons, who on account of residence, occupation or other relation, were in a position to have knowledge of the violation.

The notice to appear before the auditor, is issued in writing

16. Noval n. 776, p. 513.
17. Lega, IV, n. 303, p. 371.
18. Noval, n. 777, p. 513.
19. Instr. 1880, art. XV.
20. can. 1944 #1; 1724.

to each person (21) required to give any testimony. It must contain the name of the one authorizing it i. e. the supreme Moderator or the major Superior and that of the auditor, then indicating, at least, in a general way the reason for the appearance and clearly noting the time when to be present i. e. the hour, day, month and year together with the place, the name of the person, that is called must be also clearly indicated in this instrument (22). This instrument of citation is printed or typewritten, having the date and place where it was issued, and is signed by the auditor and his notary with the official seal affixed to it (23). Two copies are made. One is preserved with the minutes of inquiry; the other is forwarded to the person intended either by a messenger or through mail (24). The messenger, who is entrusted to make the delivery, may do so whenever the person is located. When using postal service, the letter must be registered and the certificate of acceptance or refusal demanded, in order to have evidence of the delivery (25). A record is made by the notary in the minutes of inquiry about the manner of transmitting the citation and the subsequent acceptance or refusal of the same.

The one cited to appear before the auditor is bound to obey; however, if, he is hindered in any way, it is his duty to notify the latter of the cause for his inability to be present (26). No one may shirk the duty to testify when legitimately cited, for this hinders the proper administration of justice (27). The obligation to testify, when demanded, arises from public necessity and is for common good. Those, who are called upon to be witnesses, may not withdraw themselves on account of fear, hatred or favor; if they refuse to fulfill their duty, they may be compelled under penalty to comply with the summons (28). One is not bound in justice to offer himself to testify, and if he

---

21. can. 1712 #2.
22. can. 1715 #1.
23. can. 1715 #2; Regul. Supr. Sign. Tr. a. 14.
24. can. 1716; 1717 #1; 1719; Reg. S. R. Rotae Tr. #24, n. 1.
25. can. 1719; Reg. S. R. Rotae Tr. #24, n. 3; Reg. S. Sign. Tr. a. 16; Instr, 1880, n. 14; Instr. 1883, n. XIV.
26. can. 1766 #1.
27. Schmalz., II, t. 21, n. 1; Wernz, V, n. 622, p. 471.
28. can. 1766 #2; Reg. S. R. Rotae Tr. #114, n. 4; Schmalz. l. c., n. 12; Wernz, V, n. 623, p. 471.

omits to do so there is no obligation to make restitution. However, he is bound to present himself of his own accord when his testimony is necessary to save from harm a community or a third person, which harm could not otherwise be prevented. This duty arises from charity, which binds everyone to aid his neighbor to avoid grave harm if it be possible without grave personal inconvenience. General good urges to give testimony in order that truth may not be suppressed; likewise, charity and justice require that the right of another shall not perish through a want of proper evidence (29). This obligation is not restricted to cases of extreme necessity; it is also applicable to others (30).

Those called to testify must take an oath to speak the truth in all that they declare (31). The evidence concerning the facts is not only required, but, there also must be an earnest will to manifest it truthfully and this is assured, when a witness speaks under oath. The depositions, that are produced under this security, give a convincing cogency to the assertions stated (32). Assertions, that are to the prejudice of another, are not to be credited, unless, these are made under oath (33), otherwise, they are only slight indications that have hardly any value in judicial procedure. Wherefore, the axioms "testis non iuratus non probat" and "testi non iurato non creditur" are syntheses of general laws which require that any deposition worthy of legal proof must be secured by an oath. Although, witnesses take an oath to speak the truth, they, nevertheless, may be required, if necessary, to confirm the truth of their assertions by another separate oath (34). This is done, whenever the importance of the deposition or other circumstances make it necessary e. g. when there is a discrepancy in certain answers or a serious doubt. Witnesses may be compelled to take an oath of secrecy (35) that binds them not to divulge the questions and answers given during the examination. This is especially the case during an inquiry. This secrecy binds either until the proceedings are made

29. Maschat, II, t. 21, n. 1; Wernz, V, n. 622, p. 471.
30. Wernz, 1. c. ibid.
31. can. 1767 #1; C. 39, 47, 51, X, II, 20.
32. Wernz, V, n. 637, p. 480.
33. C. 51, X, II, 20.
34. can. 1768; Regul. S. R. Rotae Tr. #114, n. 2: Instr. 1880, n. 18; Instr. 1883, n. XVIII.
35. can. 1769.

public during the trial or it may be enjoined permanently (36) if the case or proofs are of such a nature that by divulging them, the good name of others would be endangered, or occasion might be given to dissentions, scandals and other inconveniences.

Those who are examined as witnesses must be heard in the tribunal (37) or place specially designated for this purpose. The tribunal for religious is the place where their house is located (38), i. e. where the monastery is situated. The house may be a domus formata (39) or not, but it must be a habitual residence of the religious. Religious living outside of these houses are to be called by their Superior to present themselves at their respective monasteries. The Abbot, Prior or Provincial may delegate the local Superior of dependent houses to conduct the examination of religious residing at those places. When such a delegation takes place, the major Superior must also designate a secretary (40) with the examiner in order to conform with the requirement of the law. The examination is done according to the instructions forwarded for the purpose. Should deposition of a religious gravely ill at a hospital be necessary, the Superior may delegate the examiner with a secretary to hear him at the place; however, previously notification and arrangments are to be made with the local Ordinary. Religious that live in other monasteries or provinces, who cannot be easily called to their respective houses, are to be examined by the Superior of the monastery in which they live, who should be requested to do so by the Superior to whom the religious belongs (41). If, there are clerics and lay persons who have knowledge of the case, they are examined by the local tribunal upon the request of the religious major Superior or Supreme Moderator (42). The instructions and questions for the hearing of these witnesses are to be forwarded to the examining tribunal (43) according to which the inquiry is conducted; after having completed the examina-

36. can. 1623 #3; S. C. Off. Instr. Feb. 20, 1866, n. 14; Instr. (ad Ep. Ritum Orient.) 1883, t. III, n. 12.

37. can. 1770 #1.

38. can. 1563.

39. can. 488. #5.

40. can. 1585 #1.

41. can. 1770 #2, n. 3.

42. can. 1770 #2, n. 3.

43. can. 1770 #2, n. 3.

tion, the tribunal, that had assisted in this matter, gathers the proceedings and forwards the same to the first tribunal.

As mentioned before, this inquiry is conducted either by the major Superior or an auditor and his secretary. The witnesses are examined singly and separately (44). The object of this manner of examination is to avoid any danger of collusion or undue influence, which is sure to arise if there are others present. When one testifies alone, he is free from influence of human respect and other such fears that arise from presence of others and his testimony is to be believed. On the other hand a witness conscious of others' disapproval of statements that he is about to make, is apt to modify his assertions either to the prejudice or advantage of the fact. This is so true that, unless the hearing of witnesses is made singly and separately, the depositions have no value (45).

The questioning is done by the Superior or auditor. No one else is permitted to question the persons that are being examined. The notary, who is always present, must direct his queries through the examiner if, some of the answers are not clear to him, in order that he may be able to make a correct record of the depositions (46). The answers to each question are to be noted down distinctly and, as far as possible, verbatim, in order to have evidence for future eventualities; for it may happen that some of the proofs might be denied by the very persons themselves who had produced them. The records of inquiry, afterwards, will furnish ample evidence to counteract the denial (47).

The Superior formulates the questions and presents them one after another to the person that is examined. Some of these interrogatories pertain to the persons themselves, and others to the object or cause of the inquiry. The former, concerning the witnesses, are more general questions viz., the name, surname, origin, age, religion, condition, domicile, and also the relations (48) with the person under inquiry, what these had

44. can. 1772 #1; Instr. 1880, n. 17; Instr. 1883, n. XVII; Reg. S. R. Rotae Tr. #114, n. 5.

45. Schmalz., II, 20, n. 94.

46. can. 1773 #2.

47. Schmalz., l. c., n. 95.

48. can. 1774.

been in the past and what they are at the time. These questions serve not only to identify the person, but, aid in estimating the value of the depositions. The latter questions pertain to the object of the investigation i. e. the alleged existence of a transgression or violation. The order in which the questions should follow is from the general to the particular, first about the fact and then gradually concerning its peculiar circumstances or relations. The questioning must be to the point i. e. about the matter for which inquiry is held, other questions that do not pertain to the case directly or relatively are not permitted to be asked (49).

After the preliminary questions that pertain to the witness himself, the auditor, then, asks him if he has any knowledge about the fact under inquiry and if he assents that he has information, he is to be requested to narrate the facts as he knows them. Should there be suspicion concerning the sincerity of his narration, either on account of his extreme defense or severe accusation of the person, or because of his evident contradictions, he must be questioned cautiously whether he had spoken with anyone who had been previously examined, or if he had received instructions or promised not to testify etc. Besides the depositions that the witnesses produce, they must be asked about those circumstances which, perhaps, may have been omitted through inadvertance, and which may reasonably be expected to be known by them, or if they failed to explain some closely connected facts which will produce the needed indications or evidence.

The witnesses must do their best in their statement of facts. The time of occurence should be definitely stated or, at least, approximately as it is remembered; the names of persons should be given and their description, in order that they may be identified. The place also where the facts happened are to be carefully noted. Explanation ought to be given too about the causes or motives that gave occasion to violations of law. If, it be expedient, they are to be asked if they know of others who are acquainted with the same facts or who have better knowledge of the circumstances about which they were unable to give definite information (50). The origin and circumstances of evidences

49. Roberti, Commentarium de L. IV Cod., p. 573.
50. Lega, IV, n. 309, p. 377.

are to be carefully recorded by the notary in the inquiry; for consideration must be given to the manner in which knowledge of the facts was obtained, when and where it was received.

The questions are to be brief (51) so that the witness may be easily able to understand and remember them. Simplicity should be observed in the manner of questioning, in order that a witness may not be confused by a complex query and give an obscure answer. Neither ambiguous nor equivocal questions are to be asked, for these suggest a different meaning from the one intended and the answers to the same may afterwards be interpreted wrongly by the auditor himself. Subtle and artful questions must not be used, for these aim to obtain forseen responses of which the witness is unconscious and which he may be led to give. Direct questioning that would suggest answers must not be given in the very beginning of the examination e. g. if the auditor would ask, at once, about the crime and the circumstances in order that he might be able to prepare a witness for an answer. The witness must be first questioned about general things pertaining to the matter and then only about the particular (52). The questioning must be free from all offense (53).

The matter of the examination is not to be communicated to the witness (54) before he is called to testify in person. The auditor, those who had been examined previously, or anyone else, are forbidden to inform of the matter those who are to be heard. They are questioned only after having appeared at the place designated for the inquiry; here the questions are not to be given, unless, these are to be answered at once. The auditor may notify a witness, when he is cited, about some of the matter, if there be a real necessity (55), on account of the nature of certain facts e. g. remoteness of time since an event occured which could not be definitely recalled so as to be able to give a positive statement, however, great care must be taken, lest, such matter might be divulged either by a previous conferring with others or an arranged agreement to testify in a certain manner.

---

51. can. 1775.
52. Pellegrinus apud Noval, p. 343.
53. can. 1775.
54. can. 1776 #1; Reg. S. R. Rotae Tr. #114, n. 8.
55. can. 1776 #2.

The questions are proposed in the vernacular language (56). The answers are given by word of mouth which must not be prearranged, unless, there are written statements such as are recorded in books e. g. accounts, for if, time were given to make written replies, there would be opportunity to fabricate them and conceal those facts that are necessary to uncover the truth.

The answers must be written down immediately by the notary not only as to the substance, but, also as to the very words or expressions the witness may use in his testification (57). The questions need not be recorded if these had been drawn up previous to the examination, it is sufficient to number them and to append corresponding numerals to the answers given. Other questions that are asked by the auditor, must be noted by the notary in the minutes of the inquiry. Any superfluous descriptions or repetitions in answers, given by the witnesses, are to be eliminated by the auditor, who may order the notary to note only that part of the assertions which he deems necessary and that pertains to the substance of the question asked. Likewise, a record must be made whether the witness took an oath previous to his testification or if he refused to do so. Finally, all that is of any importance or that may be of use in further proceedings is to be noted in the minutes of the inquiry. (58).

When the examination is completed, before the witness departs from the stand, the entire deposition must be read to him and ample opportunity offered him to correct, add or change anything that he may think necessary (59). and according to the manner how and what is altered may be judged the value of the statements, for if, radical corrections or gross contradictions are evident, the assertions may be suspected or, at least, present indications for such grounds. Such corrections must be noted by the notary in the minutes of the inquiry. Care must be taken in such alterations, that the writing of the answers is not erased or defaced, otherwise this would offer grounds to suspect the authenticity of the depositions. The best method is to cross out the written statement in order to indicate the cancelation of the

56. can. 1642 #2.
57. can. 1778; Reg. S. R. Rotae Tr. #114, n. 7.
58. can. 1779.
59. can. 1780; Reiff., V, 1, n. 381.

same, at the same time preserving the legibility of the writing. After the final corrections are made, the testimony is signed by the witness, the auditor and the notary (60). If the witness is unable to write, he makes a sign, instead, indicated by a cross (61) in the place where he would have written his signature. A mention of this is made on the instrument itself.

The auditor may consult the Promoter of justice during the inquiry whenever he might meet with any difficutly (62). This is in accordance with right reason, for the guardian of justice is a person well acquainted and experienced in such matters, who is in a position to advise so that no injustice might be done to a third person. It is only right that the counsel of such a person is permissable, nay, even required as this assures correct proceeding in the matter. Moreover, the auditor may have two assistants or assessors (63) with whom he may consult also during the inquiry for: a) this investigation pertains to judicial matter, b) the same is the basis of the indictment i. e. through in- c) it is one of the more difficult parts of the procedure, d) finally, no one is prohibited to ask counsel, especially if the matter is of a difficult and grave nature (64). In these instances, when advice is sought from these persons, it is necessary that the proceedings be communicated in order that they may be able to know the facts and circumstances of the matter, so as to be able to give proper assistance. The law permits this (65), and it is understood, that the person to whom the matter is made known under these conditions is bound by the obligation of secrecy in virtue of his office (66).

When the auditor has gathered all evidence possible that exists on the matter for which the inquiry was made, he arranges it in order, and adds to it his own decision as to the truth of the alleged violation and the imputability of the person to whom the fact is attributed. Having signed it with the notary, he sends the whole matter to the supreme Moderator, who decides what

60. can. 1780 #2.
61. Reiff., 1. c. n. 381.
62. can. 1945.
63. can. 1575.
64. Noval, n. 779, p. 516.
65. can. 1945.
66. can. 1623.

course is to be taken (67). If the immediate major Superior has conducted the inquiry himself, he takes immediate charge of the whole matter, i. e., it continues under his jurisdiction. Either of these Superiors decides whether there is a need for further action or not according to the evidence gathered. The next step in the procedure is admonition.

---

67. can. 1946 #2; & 659.

ADMONITION

Among the proceedings against a transgressor that precede a criminal process is admonition. It is the oldest, most mild and simple means an ecclesiastical superior may employ and at times the most effective. The Gospel lays down that a brother should admonish a failing brother; wherefore, it is proper that a superior should admonish his subjects whenever they may have failed. He may, thus, more hopefully, lead back the stray sheep to the fold, "But if thy brother shall offend against thee, go, and rebuke him between thee and him alone.... and if he will not hear thee, take with thee one or two more.... ....and if he will not hear them; tell the church" (1), and again "Reprove, entreat, rebuke in all patience and doctrine" (2). This method is always to be preferred, if there may be any hope of ammendment through kind measures, before steps are taken to use more severe remedies.

Canonical admonition is either public or secret (3). It is usually employed as a remedy. Public canonical admonition is a legal admonition, while, secret admonition is paternal (4). These remedies are used to prevent or repress transgressions and violations of law. In applying them there is a certain mark of dishonor attached to the person, wherefore, previous to the application a summary inquiry must precede in order to obtain some evidence or certainty of the fact of a transgression or a violation (5).

If the inquiry, which is extrajudicial, presents grave indications of the existence of a violation, the subject is called to answer the charges made against him. This opportunity must be given him, for the proofs gathered are not final until the delinquent is heard. If he disproves the evidence against him, the matter is discharged; if he is unable to give a satisfactory explanation for his conduct, the superior may use those means which are at his disposal by common law. In this informal hearing, the superior is the judge of the matter. The gravity of the

1. Math. 18, v. 15—18; vide also Conc. Tr. Sess. 13, c. 1 de Ref.
2. 2 to Timothy, 4, v. 2.
3. can. 2309 #1.
4. Chelodi, Jus Poenale, n. 55, p. 60.
5. Wernz, IV, n. 254, p. 259; Lega, IV, n. 281, p. 351.

indications is to be measured according to the circumstances and persons that are connected with it. If the indications are not grave and the whole matter is doutful, there need be no admonition, not even paternal, but, when the evidence is grave, although not sufficient for a criminal indictment, then the delinquent must be admonished secretly (6). If the violation is established, but, it is not publicly known, the delinquent is secretly admonished.

Paternal admonition is given informally (7). The superior admonishes his subject charitably and prudently to avoid certain actions, designating even the manner and time of compliance, entreating him to conduct himself in a becoming manner, knowing that it is his duty in conscience and for his own good name and that of the community. When this admonition cannot be given personally on account of existing circumstances, it may be communicated to the subject either by a prudent religious (8) or in writing.

Paternal admonition is always secret. It is given in this manner in order to preserve the good name of the individual, especially, if the transgression or violation is not public nor sufficiently established. In administering this admonition, the superior calls the subject into his presence and also another prudent religious who acts as a witness of the fact. The religious who is a witness of the admonition does not act in the capacity of a notary. The fact of this admonition must be recorded in writing. The Superior draws up the instrument and signs it himself and the witness likewise, the admonished person may do so if he is willing. This remedy may also be intimated by a letter, when it is thus sent, the same form of attestation is observed i. e. the superior signs it with another religious. Two copies must be always made, the duplicate is placed in the secret repository of the Order. The reason for preserving an evidence of the fact is that, in case of recourse, there is a record of the admonition and the reasons or causes for which it had been made. This admonition has not the effect of a legal one,

6. can. 1946 #2, n. 2.
7. Smith, New Procedure, n. 69, p. 31.
8. Instr. 1883, n. 6.

which is required in the dismissal of regulars, but it suffices for imposing ecclesiastical penalties (9).

In order to give a legal admonition, as required by law, for the dismissal of a member of an exempt clerical religion, the knowledge of a violation of a law must be established through notoriety, extrajudicial confession or proofs that are gathered in a judicial inquiry (10). The knowledge of the fact must be established and certain.

Notoriety is of two kinds i. e. notoriety of law and notoriety of fact (11). The former is not considered here, because in order to declare a violation notorious by law, it must be declared so by a judicial sentence or confessed in a trial (12), but, the matter that we are treating here has not arrived to this stage of the procedure. By notoriety of fact is understood a violation of a law committed in such circumstances that it is publicly known and cannot be concealed by any subterfuge and the imputability, i. e. the malice with which it was done, may not be excused under any consideration (13). This notoriety may be: a) permanent i. e. the violation is continued or habitual so that the people may easily see it and know it, or b) transient, i. e. when it is done once before a sufficient number to entail notoriety or c) it is repeated when it is committed a number of times, though not indefinitely (14). In any case notoriety consists in the fact that the violation is publicly known and that the imputability of the act cannot be excused under any pretext.

Extrajudicial confession is a personal acknowledgment of the author by word or mouth or in writing of the fact of a violation made to another person outside of a trial (15). It may be made to a Superior as such, when not acting in the capacity of a judge in a tribunal. Various circumstances are to be taken into account with the confession i. e. if it is repeated and the facts agree, if the cause of a violation is known and is certain.

Finally, a violation of a law is established through proofs

9. can. 2233 #2.
10. can. 658 #1.
11. can. 2197 nn. 2, 3.
12. can. 2197, n. 2.
13. can. 2197, n. 3.
14. Schmalz. V, 1. n. 2.
15. can. 1753.

gathered in an inquiry. These consist chiefly in the attestation of witnesses and genuine documents or instruments. Witnesses must be trustworthy persons and their depositions must also be given under oath (16) in order that the fact may be established. There also may be other supporting evidence added to that of the witnesses which will confirm the existence of the fact more securely.

When a violation of a law is ascertained to exist either through notoriety, extrajudicial confession of the author himself or an inquiry (17), then the subject is called before the Superior. The Superior must have evidence of the fact of a public violation in order that he may impose a public admonition upon the delinquent. Dismissal, being a serious penalty, cannot be decreed except for serious violations of laws following previous admonitions of the delinquent. In order to admonish a subject publicly, the Superior must have positive proofs of guilt. He may obtain these proofs from any one of the three means mentioned above.

These proofs must be complete proofs. They are to be had in such a form that a denial of them is impossible and that if produced in a trial, they will suffice to secure conviction (18). A full proof is established by two trustworthy witnesses (19), also by documents or instruments. Documents are divided into private and public (20). Public documents and authentic copies of the same produce full proof for that which they contain expressly and affirm in a special manner (21). Private instruments are those that are acknowledged to be authentic by the author himself, they serve as proof against him and their attestation has the same force as that by two trustworthy persons and there is no denial of the fact to the contrary, the instrument presents a complete proof (23).

The subject, who is called or notified of the fact that there

16. Decr. May 16, 1911, n. 8.
17. can. 658 #1.
18. Noval, n. 771, p. 507.
19. can. 1791 #2.
20. can. 1812.
21. can. 1816.
22. can. 1817; Wernz, V, n. 630, p. 476.
23. Wernz, V, n. 631, p. 476.

exists a charge against him, has the right to present his personal excuse or plea. If he succeeds in vindicating his innocence, the matter is dismissed. The proceedings of this hearing are to be noted down in writing and afterwards placed in the secret repository. Should the delinquent fail to disprove the fact and the evidence is complete that a violation exists, then the Superior will employ public admonition.

This admonition is given by the Superior himself or by his mandate (24) through a delegated person. The Superior understood here is an Abbot, Prior, Provincial or quasi-Provincial (25). Whenever a Superior gives a mandate for an admonition, it is generally given to the one who had conducted the inquiry, because he is in a better position to be able to give it on account of his acquaintance with the case. This commission becomes necessary whenever the major Superior is at the same time the supreme Moderator of a religious or monastic Congregation. This seems plain from the words of the law (26) which states that after the admonitions and correction had been given in vain, the immediate Superior shall collect all the acts of the proceedings and documents i. e. the instruments that contain the evidence of the violations and the subsequent admonitions and corrections and sends them to the supreme Moderator. This implies that there are two different persons, the one who gave the admonitions and the other who has authority to proceed with the case further when it becomes necessary. Hence just as in the inquiry if the two offices are vested in the same person, the supreme Moderator must appoint someone else to give the admonition. When the mandate is given once by the Moderator, it is valid for a second admonition (27).

Public or legal admonition is given by a Superior to his subject personally or in writing. The formality necessary for this admonition is : a) it must be written; b) contain that which is to be done or omitted; c) mention the time within which it is to be done (28); d) convey opportune exhortations and cor-

---

24. can. 659.
25. Instr. May 16, 1911, n. 5.
26. can. 663.
27. can. 659.
28. can. 660.

rections; e) impose, if need be penances and other penal remedies for the amendment of the delinquent and for reparation of the scandal given (29).

The admonition, when given personally, is read to the subject present before two witnesses or a notary (30) who acts here in an official capacity (31). The admonition is drawn up on two copies giving the date and place of issue. The Superior and the notary or the two religious called as witnesses must sign it and affix to it the official seal. Whenever this admonition is conveyed by letter, one of the two original copies is sent by registered mail, and a receipt of acceptence or refusal must be demanded. The duplicate copy is placed in the repository of the Order or Congregation which is not the secret one as for paternal or secret admonition.

This admonition is public by its nature i. e. it is a public instrument which, if produced before a tribunal, will effect a complete proof (32). When it is necessary to repair scandal caused by the violation of the law, it is imposed in a public manner. In other cases, it is done in secret. On these occaisons the Superior, if he sees fit, may impose an oath of secrecy upon all those present when the admonition is given (33).

There is no more need of the threefold admonition formerly required (34). The law now prescribes that two admonitions are sufficient to demonstrate obstinacy in a subject who may be brought to trial (35). Each admonition is given for a distinct violation of a law. If violations are permanent or continual a certain time must elapse after the first admonition before the second one may be given. Three days (36) are sufficient after the first admonition, if the violation continues, in order to give another one validly. The time of the days is to be computed from midnight to midnight (37) e. g. if the first

29. can. 661 #1.
30. can. 2309 #2.
31. can. 1585 #1; 503.
32. can. 1813 #1, n. 2; can. 1816.
33. Instr. 1883 & 1880 n. VIII.
34. Decr. 1892, Nov. 4, n. 3 & May 16, 1911, n. 4; Giraldi, p. 1, sec. 643. De Angelis, III, 31, n. 15.
35. can. 660.
36. ibid.
37. can. 34 #3, n. 3; Vermeersch, Epit. I, n. 655, p. 231.

admonition is given on the 5th of January, any time during the day, the second may only follow after the midnight of the 8th. A full three days space must intervene. When violations are not continual, then admonitions are given after each commission, provided that these are more than three days separate.

A threat of dismissal must be attached to each of the admonitions (38). This is essential for the validity of the admonition has no force as a basis for dismissal, although it is sufficient for imposing ecclesiastical penalties.

The law stresses the duty of a superior to assist in the amendment of a religious, even though it may be difficult and displeasing to either. For this purpose he should, if needful, remove the delinquent from occasions of falling again even by a transfer to another place, where the opportunity is remote and the danger is minimized (39). This may be done also in order to keep a better vigilance over the individual.

In case the religious is a fugitive and the admonition cannot be conveyed to him, what is to be done? The Commission for the Interpretation of the Code, when asked about this matter, answered that provision was made in the canons of the Code which contain penalties for fugitives and apostates from religion (40). It is plain that fugitives and apostates are not subject to the regular procedure, for the penalties stated for them do not include this punishment. On the other hand the law imposes upon them a strict obligation to return to their respective religions, (41) and also obliges superiors to seek them out and receive them when they have repented of their act (42). Whenever the dismissal of a fugitive or an apostate is necessary, the religion cannot act by applying the regular procedure. It must have recourse to the Sacred Congregation of Religious, which will grant a dispensation from the usual formalities in the case (43).

A religious is considered not to have amended, if he commits a new violation or continues in a permanent violation after the

38. Can. 661 #3.
39. can. 661 #2.
40. can. 2385 &2386; Vermeersch, Epit. I, n. 659, p. 334.
41. can. 645 #1.
42. can. 645 #2.
43. Wermeersch, Epit. I, n. 659, p. 334.

second admonition had been given (44). If he wilfully violates a law anew or persists in a violation against which he is warned, his obstinacy is recognized to call for further action on the part of the religion. The law prescribes that full six days (45) must elapse after the second admonition before any further measures may be taken. This space of time serves to establish the fact whether a subject has complied with the warning or refused to do so. In the latter case i. e., if a new violation is committed, there exists sufficient evidence that a subject is obstinate. Whereupon, the major Superior carefully collects all the proceedings thus far used, and the documents demonstrating the existence of the violations and the applied admonitions, and transmits them to the supreme Moderator (46).

---

44. can. 662; Decree may 16, 1911, n. 12.
45. can. 662. Decree May 16, 1911, n. 12.
46. can. 663.

CORRECTION

Together with the admonitions that are given to a delinquent, proper exhortations and corrections should be added which are conducive to the amendment of a subject and assist in repairing the scandal that had been given (1). The amendment of a delinquent is the primary object of ecclesiastical judicial and penal system; wherefore milder means are used in the beginning and only as an extreme measure is judicial procedure employed.

Admonitions, as we have seen, are among the first means used to prevent new violations of law. Exhortations should be added to these warnings, for they are entreaties directed to the person's good will, requesting him to desist from his obstinacy and to better his life. It is a kind means that is employed in order to gain the delinquent through gentleness.

When violations of law cause grave disturbance of social order and scandal results, correction is applied (2). Public violations, that are the basis for dismissal of religious, must be previously corrected before a procedure is instituted. Here correction while being a real juridical remedy, is also a penalty in itself because it is given for a violation. If correction is prescribed by law, then a Superior must apply it, for no one should be subjected to a criminal trial, unless he has given proof that milder degrees of judicial procedure are useless (3). It certainly is more conducive to common good if trials are eliminated, and other means substituted in order to attain the desired end. Judicial procedure is not, as a rule, for the edification of others and generally is used as a last resort to maintain peace and justice.

In order to apply judicial correction, the violation must be established from positive evidence either from inquiry or personal confession (4). The superior must have knowledge of the fact such as would warrant a moral certainty. A mere denunciation is not sufficient for giving a canonical correction. The Superior ought to call his subject and permit him to give an account of himself, if he cannot disprove the evidence of the

1. can. 661 #1.
2. can. 2308.
3. Chelodi, Jus Poenale, n. 121, p. 140.
4. can. 1947.

fact, a correction is imposed. Prudence of action is required here, lest, undue zeal might cause more harm than good. Furthermore, it is to be borne in mind that the nature of a correction, as given here, is not to be a grave penalty, but, rather, a salutary punishment that will effect the hoped for amendment of the delinquent.

This correction is given by the Superior in the presence of his notary or two witnesses (5). The exhortations and punishments are to be written on an instrument which is signed by the Superior and the notary or the witnesses and the official seal is affixed to it. This is a public correction by its own nature. If it cannot be given personally, then it may be intimated by a letter. However, provision must be made for an evidence of the acceptance or refusal of it (6). It is termed judicial correction because it is given previous to a criminal trial, and because the form observed is judicial, i. e. a judicial notary is present at its execution (7). A twofold copy is made of this correction, the duplicate of which is retained in the official repository of the Order. A record of the proceedings must be kept on account of a possible recourse, or in case of a trial the matter must be forwarded to the supreme Moderator, where it will serve to determine the final procedure.

Correction is essential to determine the obstinacy of a delinquent. Should it be omitted, it may cause the refusal of the Sacred Congregation to confirm the judgment of dismissal pronounced by the tribunal against a religious (8). This correction may be given also secretly. This does not alter the nature or the form of the remedy, but the manner of intimating is conducted secretly to save the reputation of the individual. For this reason a Superior may enjoin an obligation of secrecy even by on oath upon those who assist in the matter (9). Judicial correction may be given only twice (10). If both applications

5. can. 2309 #2.
6. can. ibid.
7. can. 1585 #1.
8. Vermeersch, I, n. 569, p. 335.
9. can. 1623 #1 #3.
10. can. 1949. #1.

are disregarded, then this is a sufficient evidence of obstinacy and the case may be taken to a trial (11).

In addition to correction, penances are to be imposed (12) suited to obtain the repentance and the resolution of amendment of a delinquent (13). When imposing penances, the good will of the individual should be taken into consideration rather than the gravity of the violation (14). Moreover, the personal character and qualities are to be regarded, whether a delinquent had been guilty of violations previously and also the circumstances under which these had been committed. Penances are not directed as punishments for violations, but, rather, as means employed to obtain the amendment of a delinquent and to repair any scandal that was caused. Both correction and penances are to be selected by the Superior himself for each case individually. It must be remembered that the nature of these is not to be so severe as those that are imposed in a criminal trial (15). Among the penances that the Code prescribes are: prayers, fasting and retreats (16), others besides these may be applied, provided that they are in accordance with the spirit of the law. Correction is regarded futile if the delinquent rejects the remedies and penances or if accepting he neglects to comply with them (17).

---

11. can. 1949 #2.
12. can. 661 #1; 1952 #1.
13. Wernz VI, n. 251, p. 254.
14. can. 2312 #3.
15. can. 1952 #2.
16. can. 2313 #1.
17. can. 1953.

TRIBUNAL

The tribunal to whose jurisdiction the matter of dismissal is assigned, consists of the supreme Moderator of a religious or monastic Congregation, together with his Chapter or Counsel (1) composed of at least four religious. The tribunal, therefore consists of five members, a) the supreme Moderator and b) four religious. By a supreme Moderator is meant the superior who is at the head of a whole religious or monastic Congregation (2) directly subject to the Holy See. Under this term are included the Abbot President. Abbot General (3), Master or Minister General, Superior General, Moderator General etc., also their vicars, who have the full rights and duties of that office (4). It is to be noted, that the abbot Primate of the "Black" Benedictines is not included among the supreme Moderators here mentioned, (5) for he has no jurisdiction over any of the monastic Congregations (6), being only the Abbot Ordinary of the College of St. Anselm in Rome.

The supreme Moderator is the head of a collegiate tribunal, whose members consist of a Counsel or Chapter (7) as such. These members are constituted according to the rules and statues of each respective Order or Congregation; they are, as a rule, elected at a general chapter.

The members of this Counsel or Chapter are not to be superiors of monasteries (8). The reason for this is that they are the immediate major superiors of their subjects, and in an event of a dismissal of one of their own subjects, they would be called to perform a twofold office i. e. that of the immediate major superior, who has the inquiry and admonitions under his direction, and later on during the actual trial, the position of a collegiate judge. As it has been noted before, this twofold office is to be performed by two different persons (9). These coun-

1. can. 655 #1.
2. can. 488 #8; Commentarium pro Religiosis, vol. III, p. 39 sq.
3. Decr. S. C. de Relig. May 16, 1911, n. 1.
4. Blat. II, n. 740, p. 730.
5. Blat. II, n. 740, p. 730.
6. Augustine, III, p. 112.
7. can. 516 #1.
8. Augustine, III, p. 398.
9. can. 1941 #3.

sellors are not to be identified with the local Counsel or Chapter, e. g. they are not the members of the Chapter of the monastery where the supreme Moderator is the Ordinary. These need not be of the same monastery where the supreme Moderator resides. However, provision should be made that the Moderator may conveniently meet with them (10). Their office is for a definite period, determined by the statutes of the Order or Congregation. Generally this term ranges from three to six years according to the time when general Chapters are convened.

The persons to be selected for this office of judge are religious members of the same Order or Congregation who have been elevated to the dignity of priesthood (11), who have a good reputation, who are prudent, well versed in Canon Law, and thirty years of age (12). The question may arise whether one that is not a priest, though having rest of the qualities, could be a judge of this tribunal. The order of priesthood is not required for the validity of holding an office when to that office is not committed the care of souls (13). However, if this quality would be required for holding an office, to which no care of souls is attached, then it is only required for liceity, unless a general or particular law prescribe this expressly as a requirement (14). When asserting that the above mentioned qualities are required of members of the collegiate tribunal, we mean to state, considering the times and circumstances, that persons not having some of the aforesaid qualities i. e. especially that of priesthood or the necessary age, but possessing a good knowledge of Canon Law and moral qualities, of prudence and reputation, are not often to be found. Hence it is seen why those having the former qualities may fortunately possess the latter.

If any of the members of the Counsel or Chapter are absent, or otherwise not available the president of the tribunal (15) selects as many as are wanting to complete the full

---

10. Vermeersch, Epitome I, n. 659, p. 333.
11. vide can. 118.
12. 1573 #4.
13. can. 154.
14. can. 153 #3.
15. Decr. S. C. de Relig. May 16, 1911, n. 1.

number in the Counsel or Chapter, (16) in order that it may act validly. In choosing new members for the tribunal, the supreme Moderator must obtain the consent (17) of the rest of the Counsellors who constitute the tribunal with him (18). Even if there were only one counsellor remaining, his consent is absolutely necessary for the valid appointment of the other members; considering the extreme case when the term of all the counsellors should expire, what would be the correct action to be pursued by the president. Since there is no provision made expressly for such contingency, we think that in similar cases the matter may be solved by analogy. An abbey that is not connected with any monastic congregation has no such tribunal as the Code prescribes, consequently, the superior cannot institute a procedure for dismissal of one of its members because a competent tribunal is wanting. Now what is to be done if a dismissal is to made? Recourse is to be had to the Holy See i. e. to the Sacred Congregation of Religious in each individual case (18). In like manner we answer to the former case mentioned above, that the president must seek the advice of the same Congregation. And the latter, no doubt, will appoint a competent tribunal for the trial.

What are the effects upon the proceedings if one or more of the counsellors are incapacitated and consequently cannot remain in the tribunal until the end? We answer, if the reason for their absence is not due to an exception, then the proceedings are unaffected, for there is no substantial reason for suspecting their value on account of one or the other of the members discontinuing to be in the collegiate body. When they were in the tribunal as judges, their position was as ordinary judges on account of their membership in the Counsel or Chapter, for the law expressly states that they together with the supreme Moderator, constitute the ordinary tribunal. Here the law gives them ordinary power on account of the office they hold (19). Since they acted with ordinary power in a body, their judicial acts were valid, unless vitiation would be caused from some other

16. can. 655 #1.

17. can. 105 #1; Decr. S. C. de Relig. May 16, 1911, n. 1.

18. S. C. de Relig. May 16, 1911, n. 1.

19. Compare this can. 655 #1 with can. 1574 #1, where in the latter the synodal judges have delegated power in trials.

disregard of the rules of procedure. The substitution of others is no hindrance to procedure, i. e. for a proper comprehension of the case. This purpose is attained when the judges obtain a moral certainty about the case in order to pronounce a sentence. This certainty obtained from the evidence produced in the trial (20). Even though the whole collegiate body were changed or substituted by legitimate authority the instance remains the same (21) and the proceedings of the trial continue in their proper order. There is no need to repeat those actions which had been officially completed by the legitimate tribunal such as e. g. the hearing of witnesses or the examining instruments etc. Here it must be borne in mind, that the cause of the substitution of some or all of the members in the collegiate tribunal had not followed an exception proposed against the former members, otherwise the effects would be different upon the proceedings.

The tribunal being a collegiate body must proceed in a body (22), otherwise, the proceedings are null. An absence of one of the judges for whatever reason suspends the power of the whole tribunal. Therefore, the vacancy must be filled previous to any action taken by the tribunal.

All the members of a tribunal must be present at every judicial session, unless they delegate auditors for certain judicial acts e. g. citing and hearing witnesses (23). They must convene together at a stated time and place when deliberating upon a case (24), or when pronouncing a sentence (25). The collegiate procedure is necessary whenever any decision must be made, e. g. pronouncing an interlocutory or definitive sentence (26).

The president of the collegiate tribunal is the supreme Moderator, who cannot appoint an official in his stead because he is expressly mentioned as one of the judges (27) of the tribunal.

20. can. 1869 #1 & #2.
21. can. 1615 #1.
22. can. 205 #3; C. 16, 42, X, I, 29.
23. can. 1582.
24. can. 1871 #1.
25. can. 1874 #5.
26. can. 1577 #2.
27. can. 655 #1.

And what pertains to delegation is specially mentioned in another canon (28). His duty is to direct the trial, seeing to it that the various judicial acts are executed in the proper manner and according to the prescribed rules of the canons. He gives instructions as to the producing of necessary evidence by documents etc. Upon him are incumbent those acts which pertain to a single judge in a non-collegiate tribunal, e. g. to issue citations, to question parties and witnesses etc. However, he may delegate those acts which a tribunal may entrust to an auditor for execution. He decides what is necessary in administering justice in each case.

The president of the tribunal is to provide a Relator who is generally selected from among the judges (29); he may execute this office himself as in the S. Rota the president is the Relator (30). The appointment is to be made as soon as the case is brought before the tribunal for procedure. The duty of the Relator is to study the case thoroughly and follow it with greater care in its progress during the trial, noting down the principal proofs and the consequent conclusions, all of which he presents to the rest of the judges for their own deliberation (31). It is difficult, no doubt, for all the judges of the tribunal to make a thorough study of each case, wherefore, one judge is commissioned with this special task. Furthermore, this facilitates the progress and assures a thorough consideration of the whole matter in order that a definite and just sentence may be finally pronounced.

---

28. can. 667.
29. can. 1580. #1.
30. Lex pr. S. R. Rotae c. 21 & Regulae S. Rotae #9; Noval, n. 137, p. 75 holds that not the president but one of the others.
31. Noval, n. 137, p. 75.

DELEGATED TRIBUNAL

The supreme Moderator with the consent (1) of his Counsel or Chapter has the power to delegate a tribunal for dismissing members of the same Order or Congregation. The application of this power of delegation is limited to countries that are distant. The term, distant, has a twofold meaning, viz., the literal, by which is understood those countries that are far distant, such as the trans-oceanic, or from one hemisphere to another e. g. from Europe to America or Asia or Africa etc., the other significance attached to this term is the one derived from its relative sense by which is meant that access is either impossible or very difficult on account of existing conditions (Blat. II, n. 752, p. 737) e. g. state of war, revolution etc. In these circumstances, the delegation of a tribunal is permitted by law.

The canon requires that the number of religious thus delegated be at least three (2). However, if the supreme Moderator and the Counsel deem it more equitable, they may commit this matter to even five (3), especially when the circumstances are peculiar or the matter of its own nature is more difficult. The consent of the Counsel or Chapter must be given for the valid appointment of a delegated tribunal (4), although not necessarily by ballot.

This power of delegating a tribunal is limited to this one instance as expressly mentioned by law. No other general delegation is permitted. Herein is not contained any power to delegate an entire collegiate tribunal for the one designated by general law. Individual substitution of members against whom exception is taken by a party is permitted; the tribunal being collegiate is governed by rules laid down for such bodies.

The advantages that are concomitant with such a delegation for distant regions, are obvious viz., the matter is more easily executed, for the members are better acquainted with the country where they reside, knowing the conditions and circumstances

---

1. can. 667.
2. can. 667.
3. can. 1576 #2.
4. can. 105 n. 1; 101 #1 n. 1.

that render them more capable to judge the cases with greater equity and facility (5).

The delegated tribunal when once constituted, has full power to conduct the whole trial from the beginning to the pronouncement of the sentence inclusive (6). The whole procedure is conducted according to the same rules as those that govern the ordinary tribunal (7); for the only concession that the law has made, is contained in the different body composing the tribunal.

The supreme Moderator appoints to this tribunal also a Promoter of Justice (8).

---

5. Prummer, Manuale J. E., n. 262, p. 335.

6. Vermeersch, Epit. I, n. 660, p. 335; Fanfani, n. 405, p. 201; Prummer, no. 262, p. 335.

7. can. 667.

8. can. 1589 #2.

LIBELLUS OR INDICTMENT

After the supreme Moderator receives the proceedings and documents from the immediate major Superior, he, in turn, delivers them over to the Promoter of Justice, whose duty it is to examine them thoroughly (1) in order to know whether there is ground for an accusation or not. If there is, he will present the formal indictment to the tribunal.

The Promoter of Justice is appointed by the supreme Moderator (2), his appointment being permanent or for a determined case (3). The person appointed must be a religious of the same Order or Congregation (4). He should be a priest of good esteem, well versed in Canon Law, for the right administration of justice depends upon his proficiency, having demonstrated his interest for justice and shown his prudence in previous dealings (5). His duty is to protect justice and right, wherefore he must be vigilant over the public good in order to assist in maintaining it and prevent harm to it; for this reason, he has the exclusive right to accuse criminal violators (6). No other office may be exercised by the Promoter of Justice in the same trial (7).

He prosecutes the case personally as a party in it, proposing juridical conclusions and demanding that condemnatory sentence be passed and executed. The presence of the Promoter of Justice in criminal trials is absolutely necessary, so that, if he is not cited the proceedings are null, unless, he is present without a notice (8). Having been cited legitimately, even though not being present at some of the proceedings these are valid (9). However, subsequently, he must examine them in order that he

---

1. can. 663.
2. can. 1589 #2.
3. can. 1588 #2.
4. can.1589 #2.
5. can. 1589 #1; Noval, n. 147, p. 83.
6. can. 1934.
7. S. C. EE. RR. April 1727.
8. can. 1587 #1; Const. "Dei miseration" Nov. 3, 1741, n. 7 ,8; S. C. EE. & RR. instr. June 11, 1880, n. 13; S. C. de P. F. 1883 Amer. n. XIII; S. C. de P. F. Matrim. n. 7.
9. can. 1587 #2; S. C. de P. F. de matrim. 883, n. 11.

may make his own conclusions or suggestions concernnig the matter.

The Promoter of Justice, having received the proceedings and documents from the supreme Moderator concerning the inquiry, admonitions and correction (10), makes a thorough study of the matter; if he discovers that some of the acts either in the inquiry or the admonition were not performed according to the regulations of the law, he may if he deems it necessary, make other investigations under his directions (11), in order to obtain the necessary evidence and information on the case. The drafting of the bill of indictment or petition is an official act because it is made by a public official of a tribunal in the capacity as much.

A trial is begun by a judicial petition made by an authorized person, in our case the Promoter of Jusitce, to a tribunal, having proper competence, for the purpose of prosecuting the defendant for a violation committed against a law, subsequently notifying him of the indictment.

The bill of indictment is a judicial petition of the plaintiff containing the written charges and their causes against the defendant. It is a written instrument comprising the object of the petition with the reasons upon which it is based and the statement of what is asked of the tribunal (12). In the narrative part of the indictment the fact with necessary circumstances must be clearly indicated. The place, time i. e. the year, month, and day, even the hour should be given in order to lessen the opportunity to avoid the charge by the defendant (13) or vice versa. Together with the accusation some of the outstanding evidences must be set forth (14), although this is not absolutely necessary in order that the judge may communicate these to the defendant for his defense.

The title of the tribunal i. e. the name of the judge, the Promoter of Justice and the defendant are to be written in full.

10. can. 663.

11. can. 664 #1.

12. can. 1706; C. 1, 2, 3, X, II, 3; Schmalzgrueber, h. t. n. 2, 3, 4; Reiff, h. t. n. 8; Pirhing, h. t. n. 7; Wernz, V, n. 384, p. 313.

13. Schmalz. h. t., n. 2; Wernz, V, n. 384, p. 313.

14. Lega, I, n. 362 & 364; Devoti, can. V, n. 9.

Unless these names are clearly and definitely indicated in the instrument, the accusation is not to be sustained.

The reasons for the procedure are designated according to the nature of the violations which may be against the common law or against some special law of a religious institute.

In the conclusion, a statement of the petition may be made, which in our case is the dismissal of the member (15). It is important to mention the petition, as upon it depends the decision of the tribunal, for the sentence must conform to the bill of indictment (16).

The bill of indictment, finally, is to be signed by the Promoter of Justice, giving the date, i. e. the day, month, year, and the place in which he has his residence, in order that communications may reach him if necessary. (17).

In drafting the bill of indictment, certain qualities must be observed viz., brevity, it should comprise only necessary and useful information for the tribunal; clearness, in order that the judges may understand what is asked of the tribunal, lest on account of obscurity they reject the bill; orderly presentation of the matter, i. e. the narration of the fact or facts first, then the reasons, and finally the petition, which is the conclusion of the indictment (18).

Certain faults in drawing up the bill would justify the tribunal in rejecting the indictment. Among these may be mentioned the following; contradiction, since what is contradictory excludes itself; obscurity easily deceives, wherefore an obscure instrument must be rejected; uncertainty engenders no definite basis for an action; generalities cause an indictment to be invalid (19) ipso jure.

After the Promoter of Justice presents the bill of indictment to the tribunal, the judges must examine it as soon as possible

15. Schmalz h. t. n. 4. & Wernz, V. n. 384, p. 313; state that, in crim. cases the petition need not be made as the law already contains the penalty; however, here the penalty is not directly attached to the crimes i. e. they are only conditions necessary for inflicting this penalty, hence it seems proper that this should be expressly mentioned in the bill of indictment..

16. Schmalz, h. t., n. 4.

17. can. 1708 #3.

18. Schmalz, h. t., n. 5.

19. Schmalz, h. t., n. 5; Wernz, V, n. 383, p. 312.

and declare the acceptance or rejection of it by a written decree. The purpose of presentation of the bill is to notify the judges and the defendant of the nature of the petition. In examining it, they must give special attention and consideration to the contents and the form, and study the nature of the indictment in order to be well acquainted with the charge against the defendant. Having arrived at a conclusion, the tribunal must intimate their decision to the Promoter of Justice. Should they reject the petition of the bill, the decree communicating this must contain the reasons for this action of the tribunal (20). The correction of the bill consists in either a partial revision, i. e. rectifying the mistakes clearing the obscurities, or a complete revision of it. This, however, is permitted only previous to the plea, provided that sufficient time is granted to the accused for his defense against the charge (21). If the petition is rejected on account of the errors contained in it that are emendable, the Promoter of Justice draws up a new petition or bill and presents it again to the same tribunal (22). After examining the second presentation of the bill, the judges must again communicate their decision to the Promoter by a new decree. If they reject, new reasons must be given for the non-acceptance of the instrument (23).

A recourse is permitted against the second rejection of the bill of indictment, which is made by the Promoter of Justice to the superior tribunal, in our case to the S. Congregation of Religious, who may define the matter itself or commission a tribunal to do so. This recourse must be made within ten days after the rejection had been communicated by the tribunal to the Promoter of Justice. The time of ten days is "useful" time (tempus utile) i. e. it is not computed if an impediment exists (24) e. g. illness of the Promoter of Justice does not forfeit the right to make the recourse later, when he is able to do so. The time is computed according to civil standards, i. e.

20. can. 1709 #1; c. 15, X, II, 1.
21. can. 1709 #2.
22. Wernz, V, n. 386, p. 315.
23. can. 1709 #2.
24. can. 35.

it ends at the termination of the last day (25). The decision of the superior tribunal is final, as it admits of no further action.

In case the judges disregard the bill for a period of one month after it has been presented, the Promoter of Justice may insist that they take cognizance of it and fulfill their duty in respect to the matter. If, nevertheless, they continue to disregard the matter, the Promoter, after a lapse of five days from the second notice, (this time is reckoned as "useful"), he may take recourse to the S. Congregation of Religious (26).

---

25. can. 34 #3, n. 3.
26. can. 1710.

CITATION OR SUMMONS

The judges, having decreed that the bill of indictment be accepted, then proceed to issue the citation whereby the other party is called to be heard or to defend himself (1). By citation is meant a legal act whereby through the authority of a judge the plaintiff calls a defendant into court for the purpose of litigation (2). In a broad sense, it means a summoning of, by the authority of a judge, of the defendant, or witnesses or other persons during any part of a trial. This act of the judge is absolutely necessary for the validity of the succeeding acts of the judicial procedure, so that if it were omitted the subsequent sentence is null and void (3). This necessity has its foundation in the natural law when considered as to the substance of the act, while the form or solemnities are required only by human law (4). Natural law guarantees the right of self defense against ascribing an act prejudicial to the individual. Consequently one must be advised of the fact of indictment for the purpose of making his defense, (5) and only then, may further proceedings be taken against the defendant.

The citation is made at the instance of the Promoter of Justice, as we have seen when he has presented the bill of indictment and when subsequently the tribunal has accepted it. The judge is the authorized person (6) to issue the citation. He may have ordinary or delegated power. In the latter case it is to be noted, that the citation is to be accomplished with a copy of the delegation signed also by the notary; for delegation, unless expressly provided by law, is never presumed; wherefore it must be proven. The cited person would not be bound to appear before the tribunal were the judge incompetent because of the want of proper jurisdiction. The one that may be cited must be

1. c. 19, X, II, 2; c. 2, II, 2, in Clem.
2. can. 1711 #1; Pirhing, II, 3, n. 20; Vallensis, h. t., n. 2; Engel, h. t. n. 9; Amort, h. t. #1.
3. can. 1894 n. 1; S. C. EE. RR. Sept. 22, 1741; Devoti, Inst. can. L. III, t. 5, #10.
4. Wernz, V, n. 395, p. 321.
5. c. 8, X, I, 33.
6. Schmalz. h. t. n. 27; Pierantonelli, Praxis Fori Eccl., t. V, n. 7.

a subject, for citation is an act of jurisdiction (7). The instrument of citation contains the summons and the cause or reason for same. The cause of citation is the object of the trial, in our case, it is the dismissal of the delinquent religious on account of the violations committed by him. The Code itself mentions that the cause i. e. the accusations of the indictment, should be indicated at least in general terms (8) to the defendant when he is cited. If their nature or other reasons advise differently, the accusations need not be stated in detail (9). An indication of them is sufficient for making the citation. In the Old Law a general indication was sufficient (10), and in particular cases it could have been omitted, the only requirement being that the summons were served upon the defendant (11), and he was obliged to appear before the tribunal to answer to the charges made against him. Now it is a condition that must be observed in a citation and may never be dispensed with. Otherwise the citation is invalid (12).

It may be asked whether the bill of indictment is sent with the citation? There is no positive requirement for doing so, as it is seen, that a general indication of the cause is sufficient which contains in brief the petition presented in the bill of indictment. If particular statutes provide for this additional provision in the citation, it may be observed, for it may assist the defendant to make a prompt answer to the citation, and, for this reason the term of appearing before the tribunal can be limited to a brief period. Proofs are not to be mentioned, however, if the fact is intimated, that documents containing evidence are deposited with the tribunal (13). Delays may be prevented and the procedure of the case might be hastened.

The citation must contain the names and surnames of the judge, Promoter of justice, and the defendant. It is well if the place of residence be added to the names to facilitate sub-

---

7. Schmalz. h. t. n. 28.
8. can. 1715 #1.
9. 1880 & 1883 n. 22, 23.
10. Schmalz. II, 3, n. 20.
11. 1880 & 1883, n. 23.
12. 1715 #1.
13. can. 1891.

sequent communication (14). A citation is void if the names are not designated (15) in full as to the name and surname. Consequently no action may be taken against an undetermined person. One cited erroneously on account of a wrong name, who does not respond to the summons, cannot be declared as having been cited.

The place of the tribunal is indicated in order that the defendant may know where to appear. This is necessary when the location of a tribunal is changed at given periods of time e. g. on account of elections of new superiors and officials or when the tribunal is a delegated one. The date for appearing or answering the charges must be indicated definitely and clearly as to the hour, day, month and year (16). A reasonable space of time should be given by the judge to the defendant in order that he may prepare himself to answer the indictment. Finally the citation must be signed by the judge, or the auditor, by his special order, and the official notary. The seal of the tribunal must be affixed to it (17). Two copies are drawn up of the citation, one is delivered to the person to be cited and the other is preserved among the records of the proceedings (18).

The decree of summoning one to appear before a tribunal is an act of jurisdiction of the judicial person (19). The notification or delivery of the instrument of citation is considered as a mere act of service and not of jurisdiction, for the Code permits a messenger to enter another territory that is not under the jurisdiction of the judge as long as he deems it necessary and he gives the order to do so (20). From this it would seem that the mere act of notifying or delivering the citation is not an act of jurisdiction.

Citation is delivered either through a messenger of the tribunal or through mail. In the former case, this is done when the distance is not far and there is no great difficulty or inconvenience

---

14. can. 1708 #3.
15. can. 1723.
16. can. 1715 #1.
17. can. 1715 #2.
18. can. 1716.
19. can. 1712 #1, 2.
20. can. 1717 #1, 2.

to make a personal presentation of the instrument (21). When distance or other causes are present, then the delivering of the instrument is entrusted to the mail service (22), with the requirement that a notice of the receipt of the registered letter be sent to the tribunal, in order that the tribunal may have a record that the citation was made. The first citation is always personal, i. e. it is sent to the defendant himself (23). However during the procedure, other citations may be sent to the defendant's advocate. The defendant becomes also the lord of the litigation at the plea, and only then he may commission a substitute for himself or the judge may appoint one for him (24). The messenger may deliver the citation anywhere he might find the one to be cited (25). During the act of delivering it, the messenger signs the instrument and notes upon it the hour, day, month and year when it was transmitted (26). If the person is not found at his residence, it may be entrusted to one of the household provided that the person is of sufficient age, and could bear witness to the fact of having executed the final delivery, and is willing to do so. The messenger signs the instrument as before, but adds the name of the person to whom the instrument is given to be delivered (27).

If the person to be cited cannot be located, the judge may issue a citation by an edict (28). This is done in the form of a public order whereby the judge commands that the person should present himself before the tribunal. It is to be affixed to the doors of the court-room, for a definite period of time according to the prudent decision of the judge. It should be published also in newspapers, although, on account of scandal, this may be omitted. The publication of the edict of citation through either one of the two means is sufficient for a legal citation (29). The messenger who publishes the citation by

21. can. 1717 #1; 1880 & 1883 n. 14; Regulae Rotae #24, n. 1; Regulae Sign. A. p., a. 16.
22. can. 1719.
23. Schmalz. 1 c. n. 28; Roberti, p. 503.
24. can. 1655 #1.
25. can. 1717 #1.
26. can. 1721 #1.
27. can. 1721 #2.
28. can. 1720 #1.
29. can. 1720 #2.

edict must indicate at the bottom of the instrument, the date, i. e. the hour and day, when the citation was publicly made known, and also the duration of time for which it will exist (30).

The defendant who refuses to receive a citation is considered as having been cited (31). The messenger signs the instrument noting the date and hour of refusal and sends it to the judge (1721 #4). The purpose of a citation is to notify the person of the charges that are made against him in order that he may defend himself. However, if he refuses to accept the notice, this demonstrates that he is aware of the fact, and, consequently, there is no further need of informing him.

Every citation is a peremptory one (32); this signifies that an obligation is imposed to appear at a definite time without any further notice. If the party summoned fails to obey the first issue, another citation is necessary before he may be declared obstinate (33). After the party has been declared obstinate, the judge may proceed with the trial.

Citation is useless, unless it is delivered. The better the manner of notification the more certain the proof of having it executed. A record of the delivery must be made (34), in order to insure that the citation is known to the defendant; for upon this fact depend the subsequent proceedings of the trial. If the notification had not taken place in the proper manner i. e. either by a personal announcement of the judge himself, or through one of the official messengers or by postal service, the defendant is not bound to present himself before the tribunal, nor may he be declared obstinate for not responding to the order of the judge. The tribunal may not proceed any further in the order of judicial proceedings until it has legally notified the defendant of his duty to appear. Any act that follows a citation that had not been legally completed is null (35).

The report of delivery, being an essential part of the citation, must be made by the messenger in person. He draws up an account of the delivery stating in it the manner and circumstances

---

30. can. 1721 #3.
31. 1718 (1880, n. 24), Can.
32. can. 1714.
33. can. 1842.
34. can. 1722.
35. can. 1723.

under which he executed his duty, mentioning the place, time, person and witness etc.; then he finally signs it and gives or sends it to the tribunal, where it is kept among the judicial proceedings of the case. When the summons are transmitted through postal service, the receipt that is returned to the remitter is sufficient testimony that this remitter has delivered the instrument to the proper person (36). It is an authentic evidence of official nature and recognized by law (37).

The above is especially concerned with the citation of a defendant. However, the rules laid down are applicable for any citation of other persons, or intimations of decisions by the tribunal (38).

The effects of a citation are: the defendant who is legally summoned is bound to appear before the court or he must answer to the charges that are made against him, unless he has a valid excuse e. g. an exception (39). Otherwise, he may be declared obstinate. The tribunal obtains exclusive right to the case which was presented to it. The judges have full jurisdiction in the matter and, if they be delegated, their power remains (40), even though the one who delegated them might cease to be in office e. g. through death or expiration of his term of office. And pending the trial nothing may be done, i. e. the religious may not be deprived of his office, (41) if he hold any, on account of having been cited, unless there should be other grounds which may necessitate the removal (42). This state of affairs, when nothing is changed during the trial, remains from the citation until definition of the case i. e. the sentence (43). The sentence here meant is not interlocutory, but the final one whereby the case is concluded.

---

36. can. 1722 #2.
37. 1880, 1883, n. 14 & 1719.
38. can. 1724.
39. c. 5, X, I, 6;
40. can. 1725 n. 3; c. 20, X, I, 29.
41. can. 1725, n. 5; c. 1-3, X, II, 16; c. 2, II, 5, in Clem.
42. can. 1956; Schmalz, II, 16, n. 6; Pirhing h. t., n. 3.
43. Pirhing, h. t., n. 2.

PLEA

The citation, having been served, obliges the accused to appear before the tribunal. The cause for the appearance is mentioned already, at least in a general way, in the citation. On the day assigned, both parties i. e. the Promoter of Justice (1) and the accused (2) present themselves before the judge. The charges are read to the accused, indicating the three crimes and the evidence for the same, although not divulging the names of the witnesses, unless the accused acknowledges them to be rightly examined.. The admonitions that were given him by the major Superior are rehearsed and the proof given that these were administered or delivered, the evidence being a copy of the admonitions or the receipt from the postal authorities. Finally his wilful obstinacy is indicated, which is proved from the defect of his amendment. These charges constitute the basis of the indictment for which the penalty of dismissal is asked. This indictment made by the Promoter indicates sufficiently enough the object of the trial. However, the judge must reject any charge that is improperly drawn up (3). Consequently, there is no necessity of arranging the chapters of the charges previous to the plea, as the matter is well determined by the prosecution in his indictment.

When the parties appear at the stated time before the tribunal, the judge questions the accused upon the indictment made against him. If he denies the accusation, then the plea is said to take place. It consists in a denial of the charges made against him by the Promoter before a judge with the intention to contest the case in a judicial procedure (4). When there are several charges, each one is read successively and an answer is required for each. The notary must record the fact in the proceedings of the trial in order that the cause may be known on account of which the procedure exists. It cannot be omitted, otherwise the proceedings are null (5).

---

1. can. 1712 #3.
2. can. 1712 #1.
3. can. 1709 #2.
4. can. 1726.
5. C. 2, X, II, 6; Reiff. II, 5, n. 3.

The effects of a plea are: a) the object of the trial is determined (6). The indictment cannot be altered by the prosecution, unless the defendant consents and the judge permits such a change (7). The charges cannot be altered before the plea, otherwise, it were useless to mention the object in the citation if it were to be subsequently changed. This may be the case after a judge has issued the citation. However, previous to that, the prosecutor may be permitted to alter the indictment, if he deems it necessary on account of probable new evidence, which he may have gathered later on. An indictment is not considered as altered, if the method of producing evidence is modified, likewise, if the circumstances connected with it are afterwards illustrated, completed or corrected. b) The sentence must be pronounced in accordance with the indictment as determined by the plea (8). c) The period of producing evidence ensues and the tribunal must grant sufficient time to the collecting and presenting their proofs (9).

The case must be defined within two years after the plea had been made (10), otherwise the Promoter may appeal to the Sacred Congregation of Religious to oblige the tribunal to take action in the matter. Dilatory exceptions that regard the persons in a trial e. g. judges and the manner in which a trial is conducted, cannot be proposed after the plea, unless these were discovered afterwards (11).

Previous to the plea, a judge cannot begin to gather evidence (12) except in a case of contumacy and special necessity, when, otherwise testimony could not be obtained afterwards on account of probable death of a witness, departure or any other just cause (13).

---

6. can. 1726.
7. 1731, n. 1.
8. Reiff. II, 27, n. 77.
9. can. 1731 #2.
10. can. 1620.
11. can. 1628 #1.
12. can. 1730; C. 1, 4, X, II, 6.
13. can. 1730.

TRIAL

The plea of the accused commences a trial proper, which is concluded by a definition of the cause. The latter term signifies a formal sentence pronounced by the judges of the tribunal. The charges, as we have seen, are communicated to the accused during the plea together with the evidence. He must obtain this information in order that he may be able to make his defense. The names of the witnesses should not be communicated before the examination (1). However, the judge may do so, if he forsees no danger in possible inconveniences that might arise as a consequence. This is the reason why the names are not communicated to the adversary until the testimony is obtained (2). But whenever the names may be so communicated without any harmful effect, then these and also certain chapters, i. e. questions upon which the witnesses will be examined, are to be made known to the other party. For the latter may then be able to propose his own chapters and exceptions; these are sent to the judge who, during the examination of the witnesses, may use them according to his prudent judgment.

The judge issues a decree by which he determines the time within which the prosecution and the defense are to produce and complete their evidences (3). Sufficient time must be given in order that all the proofs may be brought forth. However, if it be necessary that the period be extended, the judge may do so, provided that it is not beyond what is equitable (4). Within this period witnesses must be cited and instruments produced for examination by the tribunal. The production of proofs is regulated by the judge in his decree appointing this period. It is successive i. e. the period is first assigned to the prosecutor to gather and present his evidence (5). Then the testimony is communicated to the accused, for he must know the basis of the accusations, in order that he may present his defense. The prosecution communicates the names and respective

1. can. 1763.
2. ibid.
3. can. 1731, n. 2.
4. ibid.
5. Bouix, II De Iud. p. 214.

domiciles of his witnesses to the judge, who cites them to appear before the tribunal for examination. Moreover, he adds the chapters or questions that he desires the judge to use in examining (6). These questions may be corrected or substituted by the judge, especially if there is a need of illustrating some point (7).

Any person may be proposed or called as witness except those whom the law expressly excludes. The testimony of witnesses is necessary for a right administration of justice in trials, wherefore, anyone legally called to this duty must obey (8). It is for the common good which demands that truth must not be concealed, lest harm might be caused in consequence thereof (9). The office of a witness is in a way public, for that reason, when he is questioned legally by a judge, he must answer (10). The law excludes some from this obligation of testifying on account of the office which they hold. These are priests in the first place. Of course it is well known that which is made known in the sacrament of penance cannot be divulged by the confessor, but besides this, he is bound to secrecy to a certain extent concerning those things which are manifested to him extrasacramentally, but nevertheless confidentially in virtue of his ministry. All those, to whom matters are confided on account of their profession e. g. lawyers, physicians, notaries etc., are also bound by the same secrecy. It is a professional secret and as such ecclesiastical law acknowledges its weight (11). Extra-professional knowledge is not included in this exception. Those fearing grave consequences either to themselves or their relatives by blood or affinity, and are related to them in any degree direct line or the first degree collateral line are likewise excluded (13). Such persons are excused from giving testimony in criminal trials, even though, they might be the only ones who are informed about the matter, for the bond of love excuses them from making depositions (13).

6. can. 1761 #1.
7. can. 1742 #2.
8. Wernz, V, n. 622, p. 471.
9. Schmalz. II, 21, n. 1.
10. can. 1755 & 1766 #2; C. 1, 2, 3, 4, 5, X, II, 21.
11. can. 1755 #2, n. 1.
12. can. 1755 #2, n. 2.
13. Schmalz. II, 20, n. 32.

Precaution is taken against defective testimony by the exclusion of persons who lack those moral or physical qualities which incapacitate them from being qualified witnesses. The only qualification required by natural law for a witness is that he has the use of reason (14). Of course any impediment that hinders the exercise of the intellectual faculties absolutely, renders a person incapable of testifying. Positive law makes several limitations in consequence of which incompetent witnesses are classified into three divisions i. e. the unfit, the suspected and the incapacitated.

The unfit (15) are sufferers from mental disorders, illness or any other impediment which prevents them from rightly comprehending or communicating facts. Those who have not attained the use of reason and those who are deprived of it are comprehended in this category. Children under fourteen and twelve years are excluded by positive law; after becoming pubescent, they may testify about matters with which they became acquainted in a time nearing puberty (16). Others who are included are the deaf, dumb and blind. These, however, may be witnesses, provided, they were in a position to take cognizance of the fact and the opposite party did not object. A sightless person is a very poor witness, for hearing alone does not suffice for testimony. Presence and sight are essential (17); however, such a person may testify if he witnessed a fact previous to his pitiable condition, because then he had the necessary qualification to perceive. For perception is the essential element to obtain and produce testimony. A dumb person may be a witness if he received the information through hearing or seeing. The deaf may testify to that which he perceived by sight (18).

The class of suspected persons consists of the following: the excommunicated, perjurors and the infamous (19) after a declaratory or condemnatory sentence. Those excommunicated by a sentence, as long as the penalty is in force, cannot act as

14. Schmalz. 1 c. n. 2.
15. can. 1757. #1.
16. Schmalz. 1. c. n. 7.
17. ibid.
18. Schmalz. 1. c. n. 8.
19. can. 1757 #2.

witnesses. Perjurors (20), even though they have repented of their act are always excluded from testifying (27). The infamous are excluded from testifying (21). The infamous are excluded from producing testimony, unless the penalty has been withdrawn (22). Although they may be permitted to testify after the penalty is removed by the proper authority, nevertheless their deposition does not effect a full proof, because they are not above all suspicion (23). Others, even though they may have committed crimes are not excluded from bearing testimony. Those of low morals by condition of life, and public enemies are excluded also from testifying (24).

The incapacitated are the parties themselves and their advocates, priests and all those who received knowledge at the occasion of sacramental confession (25). The Promoter of Justice, the accused or his advocate cannot act as witnesses, for they would be testifying in their own case which is forbidden (26).

All knowledge of whatever nature a priest had obtained in confession, even though the penitent relieved him from the obligation of the seal, cannot be used for testimony in a trial. In the same manner this incapacity extends to all those who by some chance learned anything before, during or after confession. Interpreters who assist in confession or those who simulated to hear a confession are absolutely incapacitated. The knowledge that is thus obtained has no value whatever, not even as an indication of truth.

One related to another by blood or affinity, in any degree direct line and the first degree collateral line, is incapacitated to testify (27) because of mutual love which renders the deposition suspected (28). Lay persons are not forbidden to bear witness

20. C. 54, X, II, 20.
21. Schmalz., l. c. n. 24.
22. Infamy by law may only be dispensed by the Apostolic See (can. 2295) i. e. the Roman Pontiff, while infamy by act is dispensed by a declaration of the Ordinary.
23: Schmalz. l. c. n. 16.
24. can. 1757 #2, n. 2, 3.
25. can. 1757 #3.
26. C. 10, X, II, 20.
27. can. 1757 #3; Sancti, II, 21, n. 5.
28. Schmalz., l. c. n. 29; Smith, Elements II, n. 827, p. 85.

against religious in criminal trials, especially when there are no others to be found (29) or when the testimony of other religious is not sufficient or the circumstances of the case demand that lay persons testify.

The unfit and the suspected may be heard by a decree of the judge, but in that event their testimony is only an indication pointing in favor of the proof (30). They are not required to take an oath when asked to make a deposition.

Introducing Witnesses.

First of all, when a party wishes to prove his case he has the right to present witnesses. The Promoter of Justice, moreover, as a public official, has the special faculty (31) to propose persons for testifying. The judge, also, may call any persons to testify when the case concerns public good, as in criminal trials (32). Thus the supreme Moderator may call any religious who is subject to his jurisdiction to testify; likewise, he may request any tribunal to examine such persons as there may be need.

A party who introduces a witness, may renounce the examination of that witness; however, if the other party demands, the examination must be conducted notwithstanding the revocation (33). A witness may appear of his own accord to give testimony; it is the duty of the judge to consider the motives by which he was led to do so. He may be either accepted or rejected by the judge (34), especially since testimony of such a person is not above suspicion.

Either of the parties desiring to present evidence through witnesses, must notify the tribunal of the fact after the plea, by sending the names and place of residence together with the chapters or questions upon which they are to be examined (35). The defendant or his advocate should send the chapters for the examination of both his own witnesses and those of the Promoter

29. Wernz, V, n. 611, p. 464.
30. can. 1758.
31. can. 1759 #2; Reg. S. R. Rotae #114, n. 3.
32. can. 1759 #3.
33. can. 1759 #4.
34. can. 1760 #1.
35. can. 1761 #1; Reg. S. R. Rotae #114.

of Justice, because he is excluded from being present during their hearing. The Promoter should indicate the name of those persons who are to be cited; however, since he is present during the questioning of the witnesses he may propose his interrogations through the judge then and there. If the witnesses are subject to another tribunal, this Promoter must draw up the chapters needed to enable the tribunal to conduct the examination as it is requested. This communication of witnesses is done within the time designated by the judge (36).

The judge in virtue of his legal authority regulates the number of witnesses permitted to testify (37). The names of the witnesses are not to be communicated to the accused until the publication of the testimony (38) which takes place during the proceedings of the trial or immediately before the conclusion of the cause.

Witnesses are to be cited by a decree of the judge (39). A notice is sent to each one, indicating the time and place of appearance. Everyone properly cited must present himself before the tribunal, or send a notification of the impediment that hinders him from appearing (40). Refusal to appear without a legitimate excuse or when present, refusing to answer, to take an oath or to sign the testimony, gives the judge power to compel such witnesses even by censure to perform their duty, for they are bound in conscience to assist in administration of justice.

The administering of the oath and examination is the same as that in the judicial inquiry. It must be performed by the judge or his auditor in the presence of a notary in the tribunal or a place specially designated by the judge. The judge alone questions the witness, who answers orally. Each witness is heard separately. The production of instruments also takes place during this time.

The testimony of witnesses must be communicated to the adversary in order that he may be able to defend himself (41).

---

36. can. 1761 #2.
37. can. 1782 #2.
38. can. 1858.
39. can. 1765.
40. can. 1766.
41. can. 1782; Reg. Rotae #115; C. 24, X, V, 1.

If this is neglected, the accused may appeal from the sentence (42). Publication of testimony must be made by the judge, although, it is not required for the validity of a trial (43). The judge may defer it until the rest of the proofs are obtained (44) i. e. instruments etc. However, it must be made before the discussion of the case (45). The effects of the publication of testimony are: a) the right to reject witnesses ceases (46), if it is not done within three days after the names are communicated (47). Otherwise, if done later, the party must prove or, at least, affirm under oath that the defect of a witness was not known before (48). b) The witnesses, who had already been heard, are not to be examined on the same chapters i. e. interrogations, nor are new ones to be admitted (49), unless, on account of very grave reasons which the judge must decide by a decree, having previously consulted with the Promoter of Justice. After the publication of testimony new witnesses may be heard, especially in criminal trials, so as not to prejudice the right of the accused to prove his innocence (50). Rejection is an exclusion of a witness or his testimony by a judge at the request of one of the parties (51). It may arise on account of the person, his testimony, or the manner of the examination. The rejection must be made within three days after the names of the witnesses have been communicated (52) to the other party. If the exception is admitted, the judge must appoint a certain period, generally brief, within which the Promoter or the accused must prove his allegation (53). He may leave the discussion of these till the conclusion of the case. Then all the proofs will be on hand, which may facilitate matters for deciding the rejection, as the judges will be in a better position to consider the evidence at hand.

42. C. 22, X, II, 27.
43. Wernz, V, n. 617, p. 468.
44. can. 1782 #2.
45. can. 1858.
46. can. 1783 n. 1.
47. can. 1764 #4.
48. C. 9, X, II, 19.
49. can. 1786.
50. Schmalz. 1. c. n. 126.
51. can. 1783.
52. can. 1764 #4.
53. can. 1785.

Exceptions as to personal qualities i. e. fitness, capacity and suspicion must be defined at once, when proposed. Proof for these objections is supplied by any definite evidence, e. g. presumption of law that exists against a witness on account of knowledge obtained at the occasion of sacramental confession, notorious defect such as blindness etc..

The manner of examination may be rejected if it was not conducted according to the prescribed rules of general laws. Thus an exception may be proposed if the hearing of witnesses was not conducted by a judge or his delegated auditor, or if the notary was absent. In like manner exception may be taken, if the interrogations were deceitful, suggestive, and if the verbal process of the questions and especially answers was not drawn up properly, and if any of the required signatures i. e. of the judge, notary and witness, were omitted. Then the responses may be rejected on account of the fasehood, contradiction, obscurity, want of knowledge of the facts, and the like (54). From this it is evident that these exceptions may only follow after the publication of the testimony. The judge must grant sufficient time to the party to prove the cause of a rejection (55). The proofs may be direct i. e. by positive evidence, or indirect, by producing or excluding a contrary fact which demonstrates the falsehood of that which had been asserted by the witness. He may use all means of producing evidence by witnesses, instruments etc. The exceptions may be produced orally or in writing (56). In case of the former, the notary must take a record (57) of it in the proceedings, while, when the latter form is used, the objection must be drawn upon an instrument containing the name of the judge to whom it is presented, indicating the reasons and proofs for the petition (58). It must be signed by him who produces it or his advocate, having the date and place indicated upon the instrument.

The judges must consider the matter with the Promoter of Justice and decide whether the petition is to be admitted or re-

---

54. can. 1783 #2.
55. can. 1785.
56. can. 1838.
57. can. 1707 #3.
58. Reg. Rotae #100, n. 1.

jected. If it is without foundation, or employed to retard the trial, then it is to be rejected (59) by a decree from which there is no appeal (60). But when the exception is permitted, the tribunal appoints the time for producing the evidence. If the nature of the objection is such that it must be defined judicially i. e. by producing witnesses and other evidence to substantiate the objection, the general rules, as laid down in trials must be observed (61). In the case where the incidental question may be decided without observing the judicial form, it is defined by a decree which is issued by the presiding judge of the tribunal. The reasons and arguments upon which the definition is based are to be indicated briefly (62). Although there is no appeal from the interlocutory sentence deciding an exception, nevertheless, the defendant against whom the decision was made may petition the tribunal to revoke the decision; however, the other party must always be heard (63).

Testimony received during the examination of witnesses must be estimated according to the person who had testified and that which had been asserted. The condition, character and dignity (64) of the person as witness are taken into consideration. As the condition, it is to be noted whether one is a man or woman, cleric or lay, major or minor, educated, rich or poor. For the character of a person inquiry is made whether he is honest, upright and especially worthy of trust. Dignity is estimated according to the office one holds in ecclesiastical or civil life.

Next in importance is the manner in which the knowledge had been obtained, whether it was perceived personally by sight or hearing or if accepted on hearsay, fame or credulity (65). Witnesses by knowledge are those who have taken cognizance of a fact through any of their bodily senses, e. g. seeing a person struck, or hearing a blasphemy. As these are ordinarily necessary for proving a fact (66), the cause or means by which

59. can. 1784.
60. can. 1880, n. 6.
61. can. 1840 #2.
62. can. 1840. #3.
63. can. 1841.
64. can. 1789, n. 1.
65. can. 1789, n. 2.
66. Reiff., II, 20, n. 343.

knowledge was obtained must be designated. Witnesses having personal knowledge produce complete proof in a trial, for they testify to that which they have seen or heard (67).

Witnesses of credibility are those who deduce from conjectures, indications or presumptions a conclusion about a certain fact, e. g. a person running away from a place where one is found killed creates the suspicion of guilt. Their depositions do not arise from evidence obtained by presence and personal perception of the fact itself, but through reasoning from given indications. The value of such testimony depends on the conjectures or presumptions, upon which it is based (68). These witnesses may be heard, although their testimony has not the force of a proof (69). They must be heard by the judge, but, their testimony will only be as a support to a proof.

A witness by hearsay is one who testifies as to what he had heard from other trustworthy persons (70). Such testimony received from another person has no value as a proof (71), since it is not based on the principle fact, but only on the assertion of a third person. This testimony produces only a presumption (72). Proofs by hearsay are admitted in favor of the defendant when that which is asserted was received from trustworthy persons.

Testimony by fame is based upon the opinion or belief concerning a certain fact, circumstance or its author, which exists among people of a certain place or community. Fame may arise as to person i. e. his character or particular acts. It differs from rumor or report which arises from an unknown few or a small part of a community (73). Fame as considered here is that which comes from upright persons. Its origin may be traced to certain persons who asserted that something had occured. In order that fame may have any force, it must be uniform and constant, not contradictory or indefinite. Witnesses of fame, when testifying, must indicate what they heard, and

67. Santi, II, 29, n. 29.
68. Santi, II, 20, n. 28.
69. Reiff. II, 20, n. 348.
70. Reiff. l. c. n. 346.
71. Reiff. l. c. n. 360.
72. Reiff. l. c. n. 370.
73. Reiff. l. c. 392.

from whom they had obtained the information stating the reasons or cause which gave rise to the fact. Unless these causes are indicated, it is of no weight (74). Fame is shown to exist when the names of the authors are given, who have the required qualifications to be credited, and then the cause or reason that gave rise to it (75). Fame, generally does not produce full proof or even semi-proof. It is left to the prudent decision of the judge to estimate what value it has in a given case. In criminal trials, even though it is proved to exist, it has not the effect of a proof, for the evidence produced must be definite. It must serve as an indication.

Next, the constancy of a witness is to be considered. The manner in which one testifies must be noted; whether statements are asserted with certainty and coherence, so that no doubt may arise as to the actual reality of the fact attested. However, there are those who vary or are uncertain, which qualities also must be taken into consideration by the tribunal in order to determine the value of their depositions. Wavering testimony is one that is given with a real fear or doubt, though it need not be necessarily contradictory. Such testimony is not worthy of credibility, for it is uncertain (76). If fear is only accidental, arising from the occasion of being called to testify before a tribunal, the assertions are credible, unless there should be a reasonable doubt concerning which the judge may make his own estimation. In criminal trials, wavering, vacillating and uncertain testimony has no value.

Concordant witnesses are they who testify about one and the same fact (77). Those who testify about different objects so that their assertions stand alone, are singular witnesses. These latter are divided into three classes, the adversative, cumulative and diverse.

Singular adverse testimony contains contrary assertions about the same fact as to time, place, circumstance etc.. Thus one declares that A blasphemed in a public gathering; another that he pronounced it in a school. It is incompatible that a

74. Reiff. 1. c. n. 400.
75. Reiff. 1. c. n. 404.
76. Reiff. 1. c. n. 317.
77. can. 1789; Reiff. 1. c. n. 282.

crime should happen in two different places at the same time by the same person (78). Witnesses who depose evidence about different facts that support each other, or lead to the point under controversy, e. g. one struck a cleric, another heard him boast of the fact, and another saw the indication of the blow, produce cumulative evidence (79). Again there are declarations made about different acts which do not militate against each other, but, on the other hand, do not coalesce as though one witness asserted them, e. g., one saw Titius intoxicated at A on Jan. 5th, another saw him in the same condition at B on the 9th of the same month; such are known as diverse singular testimony (80).

Now as to the value of these depositions; those which are singular adversative, do not produce any proofs, on account of the evident contrariety (81). Diverse singular testimony, although it produces a presumption and even semi-proof (82), nevertheless does not effect a complete evidence (83). Cumulative evidence that concerns different acts or indications of a committed crime, does not produce sufficient proof for condemnation; however, it establishes a grave presumption against the accused (84) upon which a trial may be begun or even some coercive remedies may be employed.

Testimony may be contradictory in two ways, according, as the witness may contradict himself or others. If a witness contradicts or corrects that which he had asserted at first before he leaves the tribunal, then his second assertion is to be recognized as true (85). For that which he had said first is to be considered to have been done through inadvertance because he corrected it at once i. e. before he left the witness stand. If he contradicts himself afterwards, outside the tribunal, the testimony given before a judge is to be honored, for it was given under oath. When witnesses contradict each other, it must

---

78. Reiff. 1. c. n. 286.
79. Schmalz. 1. c. n. 105.
80. Schmalz., 1. c. ibid.; Reiff., 1. c. n. 288.
81. Schmalz., 1. c. n. 106; Reiff., 1. c. n. 291.
82. Schmalz., 1. c. ibid.
83. Reiff. 1. c. n. 294.
84. Schmalz., 1. c. ibid.; Reiff. 1. c. n. 307.
85. can. 1780 #1; C. 7, X, II, 21; Schmalz., 1. c. n. 108; Bouix, De Iud. II, p. 316.

be observed whether they were brought in to testify for the same party or for diverse parties. When as witnesses for the same party they disagree, e. g. three testify for the existence of a crime and two, even though above all exception, against it, then the testimony is of no value (86); for in criminal cases the evidence must be firmly established. When witnesses are produced by opposite parties, e. g., three testify for the Promoter and two for the accused, the benefit is for the accused and he cannot be condemned (87).

After the plea, a period of time is assigned for the parties to produce their necessary proofs and arguments. Within this time, witnesses must be cited and instruments presented for examination, for through these evidence is established. If the time designated is not long enough, the judge may prolong it at the request of the parties (88). First the Promoter of Justice produces all his witnesses, instruments and other evidence to prove or support his charges against the accused. The witnesses are called and examined under oath one by one secretly. The instruments containing the admonitions and corrections are brought forth together with all the proceedings before the indictment.

After all the witnesses for the Promoter were heard and before the rest of the testimony is gathered or examined by the tribunal, the judge communicates the attestations of the witnesses to the accused or his advocate. The names of the witnesses are made known to the accused; however, should it be inadvisable on account of grave existing circumstances (89), then these may be omitted until the final publication of the whole testimony (90).

The right of defense exists not only by human and positive law, but by natural and even divine (91). It is of such importance that the defendant may not renounce it. For that reason an advocate must be appointed for the accused by

---

86. Reiff. 1. c. n. 322.
87. Schmalz., 1. c. n. 107.
88. can. 1731, n. 2.
89. can. 1782 #1, 2.
90. can. 1858.
91. Bouix, 1. c. p. 222; Smith, Elements II, n. 112, p. 250.

the presiding judge (92), whose duty it is, irrespective of the indifference of his client, to conduct the defense. Even if the accused confessed his violations before the judge, the Promoter is not relieved from the burden of proving the guilt (93). The accused may content himself with a mere denial of the charges as long as these are not proved. To the extent that they are supported by testimony he must advance his own proofs for his innocence. Sufficient time (94) must be given him to collect such evidence as he may wish to present to the tribunal in his own defense. At the time appointed by the presiding judge, the proofs are to be produced according to an outline of arguments which the accused has drawn up for his defense. One by one each argument is taken up and proved by the testimony of witnesses and other evidence for the accused is conducted by the judge in the same manner as it was for the Promoter of Justice. Just as the accused may present objections to the witnesses and their testimony presented by the Promoter, so also the latter may take exception to those of the former (95). The Promoter is present during the examination of witnesses (96). He may direct his interrogations through the judge instructor. who will examine them upon these suggestions. This is known as cross examination.

After all the witnesses, instruments and documents which the parties produced are examined and there is no more evidence to be offered, the judge orders the publication of all the proofs collected during the examination of the evidence of both parties. This must be done before the final discussion i. e. the written defense (97) is made. The instrument of this publication contains the various steps of the judicial proceedings i. e. the indictment, citation, plea, examination of witnesses and instruments and all the arguments which were adduced by both parties. The evidence of the Promoter of Justice is drawn up first and then that of the accused (98). The publication of the entire process

92. can. 1655 #1.
93. can. 1751.
94. can. 1862 #1.
95. can. 1764 #4; Schmalz. II, 20, n. 123
96. can. 1773 #2.
97. can. 1866.
98. Smith, New Procedure, n. 391, p. 163.

is a mutual communication of all the proceedings and proofs to the parties by the tribunal. It enables them to study and compare their respective evidence in order to prepare and formulate their final defense.

When all the proofs from witnesses, instruments and other legal means are completed, the cause is closed (99). This is done after the time appointed for producing evidence (100) has expired, or the judge relator declares that the case is sufficiently established i. e. that there are sufficient proofs on hand (101). This act of concluding the case is declared by a decree of the judge relator (102). After the closing of the case further evidence is not permitted, unless new documents or instruments are found, or unless witnesses, who were impeded during the time prescribed for the hearing, are now able to present themselves (103). However, if there is a grave cause or reason for permitting new proofs, the judge relator may allow these to be admitted. The other party must be informed and heard concerning the matter, in order that it may have an opportunity to defend itself either by taking exception or by producing counter proofs. Sufficient time must be granted to the accused to enable him to collect new proofs for a rebuttal. If this right were denied, the trial thereby would be nullified (104). The judge in virtue of his office, may cite and question both parties any time during the trial. As it is his duty fully to study and investigate the case, he may seek information by questioning those connected with the case whenever there may arise any doubt concerning it (105).

Following the closing of the cause, the judge relator assigns a suitable time to the parties to sum up their defense (106). This is a written (107) disputation whereby the evidence of the opossing party is impugned. The parties argumentation rests upon the facts of the proceedings and proofs which were com-

---

99. can. 1860 #1.
100. can. 1731, n. 2.
101. can. 1860 #2.
102. can. 1860 #3.
103. can. 1861 #1.
104. can. 1861 #2.
105. Noval, n. 611, p. 404.
106. can. 1862 #1.
107. can. 1863 #1.

municated to them at the conclusion of the cause. This summing up of the defense is to demonstrate that the evidence produced during the trial established beyond doubt either the guilt or the innocence of the accused (108). The Promoter of Justice will attempt to prove that the accused is guilty, whereas the accused will endeavor to prove himself to be innocent.

The Promoter of Justice and the advocate shall review the whole procedure and the evidence brought forth, and compare these in view of the existing law. Thus they will be able to deduce definite conslusions concerning the evidence at hand either for a condemnation or a discharge. The advocate will endeavor to prove at least some of the following points, a) that the alleged violations were never committed; b) even if perhaps they were, the evidence is not sufficint; c) granted that the existence is established, the author of the transgression is not absolutely determined; d) although it is not positively proved that the defendant is guiltless, it is evident that there is no legitimate and sufficient proof for the crime, because of the following causes: a) the proceedings are null, b) the witnesses were incapacitated to testify, c) testimony is contradictory and consequently did not establish the existence of the violations or the obstinacy of the accused. Finally, if the truth of those charges is proved, the imputability is not certain for it was not committed with the required malice (109). The advocate, having proved anyone of these arguments, demands in conclusion the discharge of his client. If the period for defense is too brief, it may be prolonged by the presiding judge upon the request of one of the parties; however, the other party must always be notified of the fact (110).

The final defense of the Promoter of Justice and the accused is issued in writing (111). The presiding judge may order these to be printed or typewritten, together with the principal instruments or documents, the whole being then bound in pamphlet form (112). The substantial arguments are to be drawn up in a

108. Smith, New Procedure, n. 416, p. 175.
109. Bouix. l. c. p. 587.
110. can. 1862 #2.
111. can. 1863 #1.
112. can. 1863 #3; Reg. S. R. Rotae #45.

brief, but clear form. A summary of the proceedings is to be included in these pamphlets. Before the matter is submitted for printing, the manuscripts of the parties must be shown to the judge relator, who will direct what is to be printed. He also decides what documents and proceedings are to be included. Care must be taken that the matter is not made publicly known in any way. A copy of this printed defense must be given to each judge (113), to the Promoter of Justice and to the accused (114).

After the defense is communicated to the parties, each one is permitted to reply. This reply must be made in writing within the time designated by the presiding judge (115). This right of replying to the defense is permitted only once. However, if there are grave reasons, the judge may allow another rejoinder (116).

Oral information is forbidden to the advocate (117). Such personal private interviews with a judge or judges tends to influence their opinion which should be impartial. A limited discussion for the purpose of illustrating some special or more difficult questions may be permitted in the presence of one of the judges, who represents the tribunal (118). A general peroration of the whole cause is not allowed (119). Previous to the discussion, the parties must present a brief outline of the points or questions in writing which they desire to argue. The presiding judge shall communicate these to the parties and designate the day and hour for the discussion (120). Besides the judge, who has charge of the discussion, a notary of the tribunal must be appointed to be present and record those proceedings which the judge may order or the parties may request to be noted (121). Otherwise the matter has no juridical value, if it is not recorded by a notary.

---

113. can. 1863 #1.
114. can. 1863 #2.
115. can. 1865.
116. can. 1865 #2; Reg. S. R. Rotae #50, n. 1.
117. can. 1866 #1.
118. can. 1866 #2.
119. Noval n. 616, p. 406.
120. can. 1866 #3.
121. can. 1866 #4.

SENTENCE

After the final defense and discussion when all the evidence for and against the cause were sufficiently argued, a sentence must be pronounced (1). Sentence is a legitimate pronouncement whereby a judge defines a cause that had been proposed by the litigants and judicially contested (2). When the pronouncement decides the main issue, then it is a definitive sentence; if an incidental question i. e. an exception is determined, then it is an interlocutory sentence. In order that a judge may pronounce a sentence he must have moral certainty regarding the matter to be decided (3). Moral certainty is defined as "infirma mentis adhaesio alicui propositioni absque formidine errandi" (4). This intimate conviction is obtained from the proceedings and proofs of the trial (5). Only that information and evidence which were produced in the trial may serve as source for convincing the judges. Private, extrajudicial knowledge is absolutely excluded (6). The judges must estimate the proofs according to their own conscience, unless the law expressly determines the value of the same (7). Their value is determined in the light of reason whether these produce complete or partial testimony or none at all. The law defines the force of certain proofs e. g. two sworn witnesses, who are above all exception, produce a complete proof (8), also public instruments concerning that which is directly and principally affirmed in them (9). This conviction or certainty refers not only to the existence or truth of the facts or proofs, but, also regards the justice of the sentence(10). If a judge is unable to attain to moral certainty, he must dismiss the accused (11). This in-

---

1. can. 1870.
2. can. 1868 #1.
3. can. 1869 #1.
4. As Noval, n. 620, p. 409.
5. can. 1869 #2.
6. As DeLuca, De Iud., disc. 22, n. 2 sq. apud Smith, New Procedure, n. 420, p. 178.
7. can. 1869 #3.
8. can. 1791 #2.
9. can. 1816.
10. Noval, n. 624, p. 412.
11. can. 1869 #4.

ability may arise from a want of proper proofs having the necessary efficacy of producing real i. e. subjective or legal i. e. objective conviction. However, if there are full proofs the judge must pronounce a sentence according to them as the law ordains (12). Sufficient time must be granted to the judges to prepare their conclusions. Each one reviews carefully the evidence of the prosecution and the defense and prepares his decision on the case.

The president of the tribunal appoints a day and hour for a meeting of the collegiate tribunal in order to deliberate and decide upon the case (13). This convening of the tribunal is secret, for the judges alone are present (14). Having convened on the day appointed, the judge relator, whose duty it is to study the case thoroughly, presents a writen summary of the entire case indicating all the leading proofs and counter-proofs with the consequent conclusion and arguments therefor. Each one of the other judges produces in writing his own conclusion or decision with brief proofs or reasons deduced from law or fact. A moderate discussion of the case follows under the direction of the president of the tribunal. Here they compare their decision and reasons upon which these are based. They may correct and make suggestions upon the matter (15). Although the judges have decided upon a conclusion before this consultation, nevertheless, anyone may relinquish his former decision and agree upon a new one, if he is prompted by just reasons (16). If an agreement is not reached in the first discussion, the decision may be deferred for another meeting of the tribunal, which should not be prorogued beyond a week (17). A decision is arrived at, when the collegiate tribunal agree on a sentence by an absolute majority vote (18).

This sentence is either condemnatory or absolutory. If the charges i. e. the three violations and obstinacy, are proved to

---

12. can. 1869 #3.
13. can. 1871 #1.
14. Reg. S. R. Rotae #177, n. 1.
15. Smith Elements II, n. 1143, p. 258.
16. can. 1871 #4.
17. can. 1871 #5.
18. can. 101 #1, n. 1.; Reg. S. R. Rotae #176; Lex pr. S. R. Rotae & Sign. Ap. can. 31 #3.

exist from the arguments and proofs produced in the trial by the Promoter of Justice, the sentence of dismissal is pronounced against the accused religious. Should the prosecution fail to establish the existence of these facts, the tribunal must pronounce in favor of the accused. The sentence must contain the reasons upon which it is based (19). These motives or reasons are drawn up from those which the judges had produced during the discussion (20).

The sentence is drawn up in writing, which commences with the divine invocation. The names of the judges of the tribunal, of the Promoter of Justice, and of the accused, together with the place of residence, must be expressed. Then the charges are briefly enumerated with the final conclusions and the reasons for same. In conclusion, the date and place where it was issued, are indicated and signed by all the judges of the collegiate tribunal and the notary (21).

The sentence is then published as soon as possible (22). The parties are cited to appear at a certain date before the tribunal in order to hear the solemn reading of the sentence. The presiding judge pronounces it in the name of the tribunal. It may also be made known to the accused by transmitting it through postal service (23). The missive must be registered in order to insure certain delivery. If the religious is condemned, he may appeal within ten days after the notification of the sentence to the Sacred Congregation of Religious (24).

The sentence cannot be carried out into effect, unless it is confirmed by this Congregation (25). For this purpose, the president of the tribunal shall send all the proceedings of the trial to it. After the ratification, the sentence is to be executed according to the instructions that this Congregation may have prescribed.

---

19. can. 1873 #3.
20. can. 1872 #2; Reg. S. R. Rotae #187.
21. can. 1874.
22. can. 1876.
23. can. 1877.
24. can. 1881.
25. can. 666.

CONCLUSION

It must impress even the casual reader what great care the Church has devoted to establish a judicial system for the proper administration of justice. The principles and modes of procedure have been so wisely defined that there is no possibility for an innocent party to be condemned. She sees to it that even the guilty one shall receive every opportunity for defense. Only after a thorough and painstaking trial, when the tribunal is convinced of the guilt of the accused a judgment is pronounced.

BIBLIOGRAPHY

SOURCES.

Acta Apostolicae Sedis, Romae, 1909-1923.
Acta Sanctae Sedis, Romae, 1865-1908.
Analecta Ecclesiastica, Romae, 1893-1911.
Bullarium Romanum, Augustae Taurinorum, 1868.
Canones et Decreta Sacro sancti Oecumenici Concilii Tridentini, Romae, 1904.
Codex Iuris Canonici, Pii X, Pontificis Maximi, Iussus Digestus, Benedicti Papae XV, Autoritate Promulgatus, Romae, 1918.
Collectanea Sacrae Congregationis de Propaganda Fide, Romae, 1907.
Corpus Iuris Canonici, editio Lipsiensis secunda, Richter-Friedberg, Lipsiae, 1922.
Holy Bible, The, Baltimore, 1914.

AUTHORS.

Amort, Eusebius, Elementum Iuris Canonici Veteris et Moderni, Ferrariae, 1763.
Augustine, Charles, O. S. B., A Commentary on Canon Law, St. Louis, 1918-1922.
Arynhac, H. A., S. S., Penal Legislation in the New Code of Canon Law, New York, 1920.
Benedict XIV, De Synodo Diocesana, Romae, 1806.
Bizzarri, Andreas, Collectanea in usum Secretariae Sacrae Congregationis Episcoporum et Regularium, Romae, 1885.
Blat, Albertus, O. P., Commentarium Textus Codicis Iuris Canonici, Liber II, De Personis, Romae, 1919.
Bouix, Tractatus de Iudiciis Ecclesiasticis, Parisiis, 1884.
Cavagnis, Felix, Institutiones Iuris Publici Ecclesiastici, Romae, 1882.
Cavigioli, Johannes, De Censuris Latae Sententiae, Torino, 1918.
Chelodi, Ioannes, Ius Poenale, et Ordo Procedendi in Iudicis Criminalibus, iuxta Codicem Iuris Canonici, Tridenti, 1920.
Commentarium pro Religiosis, Romae, 1920-1923.
Constitutiones Fratrum Sancti Ordinis Praedicatorum, Parisiis, 1886.
D'Annibale, Iosephus, Summula Theologiae Moralis, Romae, 1908.
De Angelis, Philippus, Praelectione Iuris Canonici, Romae, 1879.
Devoti, Ioannes, Institutiones Canonicae, Leodii, 1860.
Droste, Francis, Canonical Procedure in Disciplinary and Criminal Cases of Clerics, New York, 1887.
Engel Ludovicus, O. S. B., Collegium Universi Iuris Canonici, Beneventi, 1760.
Fanfani Ludovicus, O. P., De Iure Religiosorum, Augustae Taurinorum, 1920.
Ferraris, F. Lucii, O. M., Reg. Obs. Sti. Francisci, Bibliotheca Canonica, Iuridica, Moralis, Theologica nec non Ascetica, Polemica, Rubricistica, Historica, Romae, 1885-1892.

Fagnanus, Prosper, Commentarium in V Libros Decretalium, Venetiis, 1729.
Giraldi, Ubaldus, O. Sch. P., Expositio Iuris Pontificii, Romae, 1829.
Lega, Michael, De Iudiciis Ecclesiasticis, Romae, 1901.
Leurenius, Petrus, S. I., Forum Ecclesiasticum, Venetiis, 1729.
Maschat, Remigius, O. Sch., P., Institutiones Canonicae, Romae, 1757.
Noldin, H., S. I., - Schoenegger, A., S. I., D ePoenis Ecclesiasticis, Oeniponte, 1921.
Noval, Iosephus, O. P., Commentarium Codicis Iuris Canonici, Liber IV, De Processibus, Romae, 1920.
Pierantonelli, Pacificus, Praxis Fori Ecclesiastici, Romae, 1883.
Pirhing, Enricus, S. I., Ius Canonicum, Dilingae, 1722.
Polmano, Ioannes, Brevarium Theologicum, Mediolani, 1873.
Pruemmer, Dominicus, O. P., Manuale Iuris Ecclesiastici, Friburgi Brisgoviae, 1920.
Reiffenstuel, Anacletus, O. F. M., Ius Canonicum Universum, Venetiis, 1735.
Sabetti-Barret, Compendium Theologiae Moralis, New York, 1919.
St. Augustine, Regula, Averbode Abbey, Belgium, 1898.
St. Basil, Opera omnia, Parisiis, 1839.
St. Benedict, The Holy Rule, Atchison, Kans., 1912.
St. Thomas, Summa Theologica, Romae, 1894.
Santi, Fracniscus, Praelectiones, Iuris Canonici, New York, 1886.
Schmalzgrueber, Franciscus, S. I., Ius Ecclesiasticum Universum, Ingolstadii, 1728.
Schmier, Franciscus, O. S. B., Iurisprudentia Canonico Civilis seu Ius Canonicum Universum, Venetiis, 1754.
Smith, S. B., Elements of Ecclesiastical Law, New York, 1882.
Smith, S. B., The New Procedure in Criminal and Disciplinary Cases of Ecclesiastics, New York, 1888.
Sole, Iacobus, De Delictis et Poenis, Romae, 1920.
Suarez, Franciscus, S. I., Opera Omnia, Parisiis, 1866.
Vallensis, Andrea, Paratitla Iuris Canonici sive Decretalium, Venetiis, 1732.
Vermeersch, Arthurus, S. I., Epitome Iuris Canonici, Mechlinae, 1921.
Vermeersch, Arthurus, S. I., De Religiosis Institutis et Personis, tom. II., Brugis, 1909.
Vermeersch, Arthurus, S. I., De Religiosis et Missionariis, Periodica, Brugis, 1911-1923.
Wernz, Franciscus, S. I., Ius Decretalium, Prati, 1911-1915.

UNIVERSITA CATHOLICA AMERICAE

WASHINGTONII, D. C.

SACRA FACULTAS THEOLOGICA

1922—1923

No. 19

DEUS LUX MEA

CANONES

quos

AD DOCTORATUS GRADUM

in

JURE CANONICO

apud

UNIVERSITATEM CATHOLICAM AMERICAE

Consequendum
Publice Propugnabit

WENCESLAUS CYRILLUS MICHALICKA, O. S. B.,
Abbatiae S. Procopii apud Lisle, Illinois
Juris Canonici Licentiatus.

HORA X. A. M. DIE XXVIII. MAII A. D. MCMXXIII

I	Canones 1-7	Proemium ad "Normae Generales".
II	Canones 8-14	De Legis Canonicae Indole et Subiecto.
III	Canones 15-21	De Legis Canonicae Effectibus et Interpretatione.
IV	Canones 22-24	De Legis Canonicae Cessatione.
V	Canones 30-35	De Temporis Supputatione
VI	Canones 36-47	De Auctore, Subiecto et Valore Rescriptorum.
VII	Canones 48-59	De Rescriptorum Praecedentia, Interpretatione et Exsecutione.
VIII	Canones 60-61	De Duratione et Cessatione Rescriptorum.
IX	Canones 80-86	De Dispensationibus.
X	Canones 90-95	De Domicilio et Quasi-Domicilio.
XI	Canones 111-117	De Incardinatione et Excardinatione.
XII	Canones 118-123	De Iuribus et Privilegiis Clericorum.
XIII	Canones 196-198	De Potestate Ordinaria.
XIV	Canones 199-210	De Potestate Delegata.
XV	Canones 215-217	De Divisione Diocesis.
XVI	Canones 518-520	De Confessariis et Cappellanis Ordinariis.
XVII	Canones 521-530	De Confessariis Extraordinariis.
XVIII	Canones 572-578	De Professione Religiosa.
XIX	Canones 587-591	De Ratione Studiorum in Religionibus Clericalibus.
XX	Canones 637-645	De Dimissione Religiosorum Votorum Temporarium.
XXI	Canones 654-668	De Processu Iudiciali in Dimissione Religiosorum Religionis Clericalis Exemptae.
XXII	Canones 762-769	De Patrinis in Baptismo.
XXIII	Canones 777-779	De Collati Baptismi Adnotatione et Probatione.
XXIV	Canones 872-892	De Ministro Sacramenti Poenitentiae.
XXV	Canones 593-900	De Reservatione Peccatorum.
XXVI	Canones 908-910	De Loco ad Confessionis Excipiendas.
XXVII	Canones 973-982	De Requisitis in Subiecto Sacrae Ordinationis.
XXVIII	Canones 992-1001	De Iis Quae Sacrae Ordinationi Praeire Debent.
XXIX	Canones 1012-1015	De Natura Matrimonii Eiusque Divisione.
XXX	Canones 1043-1046	De Potestate Dispensandi Urgente Mortis Periculo
XXXI	Canones 1060-1064	De Impedimento Mixtae Religionis.
XXXII	Canones 1070-1071	De Impedimento Disparitatis Cultus.
XXXIII	Canones 1094-1103	De Forma Celebrationis Matrimonii.
XXXIV	Canones 1247-1249	De Diebus Festis.
XXXV	Canones 1349-1351	De Sacris Missionibus.
XXXVI	Canones 1372-1383	De Scholis.
XXXVII	Canones 1572-1579	De Iudice Primae Instantiae.
XXXVIII	Canones 1580-1584	De Auditoribus et Relatoribus.
XXXIX	Canones 1585-1590	De Notario, Promotore Iustitiae et Vinculi Defensore.
XL	Canones 1594-1596	De Tribunali Secundae Instantiae.

XLI Canones 1606-1607 De Tribunali Delegato.

XLII Canones 1656-1666 De Procuratoribus ad Lites et Advocatis.

XLIII Canones 1706-1710 De Libello Litis Intorductorio.

XLIV Canones 1711-1725 De Citatione et Demuntiatione Actorum Iudicialium.

XLV Canones 1726-1731 De Litis Contestatione.

XLVI Canones 1756-1758 Qui Testes Esse Possunt.

XLVII Canones 1767-1769 De Iureiurando Testium.

XLVIII Canones 1770-1781 De Examine Testium.

XLIX Canones 1789-1791 De Testimoniorum Fide.

L Canones 1868-1877 De Sententia.

LI Canones 1939-1946 De Inquisitione Iudiciali.

LII Canones 1947-1953 De correptione Delinquentis.

LIII Canones 2195-2198 De Natura Delicti Eiusque Divisione.

LIV Canones 2226-2235 De Subiecto Coactivae Potestati Obnoxio.

LV Canones 2245-2247 Reservatione Censurarum.

LVI Canones 2248-2254 De Absolutione Censurarum.

LVII Canones 2306-2311 De Remediis Poenalibus.

LVIII Canones 2368-904 De Poenis in Solicitantes.

LVIX Can. 2369-889-890 De Poenis in Violantes Sigillum Sacramentale.

LX Canones 2385-2386 De Delictis contra Obligationes Proprias Status Religiosi.

Vidit Sacra Facultas:

CAROLUS F. AIKEN, S.T.D., p. t. Decanus

H. SCHUMACHER, S.T.D., p. t. a Secretis

Vidit Rector Universitatis:

† THOMAS J. SHAHAN, S.T.D., J.U.L., LL.D.

VITA.

Wenceslas Cyrill Michalicka was born near Union City, (Okla. (Ter.), April 26, 1894. He received his elementary education in country and parochial schools. His secondary and junior college education was obtained at St. Procopius Academy and College, Lisle, Ill., whereupon he entered the Benedictine Order in 1913. After his religious profession he persued the prescribed courses in philosophy and theology at St. Procopius Seminary, Lisle, Ill., and was ordained May 29, 1920. In autumn of the same year he entered the Catholic University of America and attended the lectures of Rt. Rev. Philip Bernardini, S. T. D., J. U. D., in Canon Law, of the Very Rev. Charles Francis Aiken, S. T. D., in Apologetics, and of the Rev. William Kerby, L. L. D., in Sociology.

The author takes this occasion to acknowledge his indebtness and desires to express his sincerest gratitude to his professors and the members of the Faculty of Sacred Sciences.

www.ingramcontent.com/pod-product-compliance
Lightning Source LLC
LaVergne TN
LVHW050158080826
844660LV00012B/315

* 9 7 8 0 8 1 3 2 2 2 1 0 3 *